GOD OF OUR WEARY YEARS

The Reconciliation of Race and Faith

For Aaron,

M J Cushman

11/14/10

Dr. M. Tyrone Cushman

ISBN: 978-1-4276-5011-5
Library of Congress Control Number: 2010927378

Acknowledgements

To my wife of forty-two years, Jackie, my childhood sweetheart, with whom my childhood dreams of life, love, family, and writing this book have all come true.

To Carmen, Michael, Karen, Paul, and Tam, my children, for whom there are no words to describe my love, my pride, and the honor of being called Dad.

To my mother, Vivian Beatrice Johnson-Cushman, who taught me to speak and to think, who left to me her legacy and love of expressing feelings with words, who introduced me to Jesus, and who taught me unconditional love.

To the Wisconsin Avenue Church of God, the womb from which I emerged the second time and grew up to love God's church.

To Dr. Rita Joyce Johnson, my mentor, my sister, my heroine, my friend. Your encouragement and your sharing of trust and treasure knew no boundary. I owe you.

To Ann Small-Roseboro my long and dear friend who took the raw draft and made the crooked places straight.

To my editor Brenda Pitts, my gift from God, whose professionalism and spirit matched mine; whose criticisms, corrections and suggestions helped shape this first book.

To Elena, Leslie and Destiny "Poppie's Angels" you are our hope for tomorrow. You will be the "free generation". I promise to leave you a better world.

Finally, to my mentor, the late Bishop Benjamin F. Reid, who urged me to preach, pastor, and write, who was the iron that sharpened my iron, and who poured out until there was no more.

CONTENTS

Part 1
The Spirit of Division

Part 3
Strategies and Applications

Preface

God of Our Weary Years

Almost every year of my twenty-two years as senior pastor of the Pasadena Church of God, we, like most African American congregations across this great nation, celebrated the last Sunday in February (African American history month) by dressing in traditional African clothing. We celebrated the generations that survived slavery. We mourned those martyrs of movements, marches, and uprisings that made celebration possible. Our singing and preaching connected us to our history, memorialized "the Struggle," and promoted the hope of a more perfect union.

Perhaps the greatest highlight and the most anticipated event of the day was the singing of what some call the Negro national anthem. On this special day, along with the hymns of the church and the exciting celebratory rhythms of contemporary gospel, a most sacred moment came when we stood to our feet to reverently sing James Weldon Johnson's "Lift Every Voice and Sing."

The moment the Hammond B3 sounded the introduction, the reverent rustle of the audience standing to its feet swept through the building. All eyes forward, we sang our best, each verse swelling in sweet and holy harmony towards the next. It never failed; the second verse almost always brought weeping:

Stony the road we trod,
Bitter the chast'ning rod,
Felt in the days when hope unborn had died;
Yet with a steady beat,
Have not our weary feet
Come to the place for which our fathers sighed?
We have come over a way that with tears has been watered,
We have come, treading our path through the blood of the slaughtered,
Out from the gloomy past,
'Til now we stand at last
Where the white gleam of our bright star is cast.

The final verse was sung acappella. The harmonies, always rich and precise, reverberated with clear and awesome African sound, creating a moving, sacred atmosphere that begged for the silence that followed. We sang to "them": our parents, grandparents, great-grandparents, and greater yet. Even those born after the struggle of the sixties could sense the heaviness of the moment; and without hesitation, from memory and in perfect four-voice harmony, we all sang in honor of ancestors and martyrs described in the lyrics:

God of our weary years,
God of our silent tears,
Thou who has brought us thus far on the way;
Thou who has by Thy might
Led us into the light,
Keep us forever in the path, we pray.
Lest our feet stray from the places, our God, where we met Thee,
Lest our hearts, drunk with the wine of the world, we forget Thee;
Shadowed beneath Thy hand,
May we forever stand,
True to our God,
True to our native land.

Every year I would follow that verse with a tearful plea to our young to not waste the blood, tears, and suffering of those who had died in faith believing. I reminded them of the price that had already been paid — the debt owed — and that we still have a ways to go before we can sleep.

At the risk of careers and life itself, frontline warriors embedded in the humiliating give-and-take of human struggle have always chronicled their journeys and taken their stories to whoever would listen. Through poetry and prose, music and op-ed pieces, they have laid bare soul-felt pain and head-bowing shame, with the hope that right-thinking human beings would read, weep, and start the revolution.

Through quaint melodies and coded lyrics sung while sweating and bleeding, these men and women gave voice to millions of silent screams. They were heroes and "she-roes," unheralded in history and unnoticed in headline or byline, whose music, a lullaby to the unsuspecting watchman who believed at his peril that singing slaves were happy slaves, announced the time of their deliverance, like the ominous gong of the chapel bell:

> *The Gospel train's a'comin'*
> *I hear it just at hand*
> *I hear the car wheel rumblin'*
> *And rollin' thro' the land*

> Chorus:

> *Get on board little children*
> *Get on board little children*

Get on board little children
There's room for many more

I hear the train a'comin'
She's comin' round the curve
She's loosened all her steam
And brakes And strainin' ev'ry nerve

Chorus:

The fare is cheap and all can go
The rich and poor are there
No second class aboard this train
No difference in the fare

Many think that Curtis Mayfield's powerful 1965 rendition was inspired by this anonymous original:

People get ready
There's a train a-coming,
You don't need no ticket,
You just get on board.

Indeed, the freedom train rolled on the first full moon of any given night. It heralded the beginning of an emancipation that could not wait for the conflicted declaration of Abraham Lincoln. There were no train whistles or celebratory send-offs for those courageous passengers. They stole away quietly, disappearing into dark night swamps and moonlit bayous, heading for hope in another place — somewhere, anywhere but there.

Silent Screams

One of the most unforgettable scenes ever caught on film is the last episode of the Academy Award–winning *The Godfather*. Frozen in time is the twenty-second silent scream of Michael Corleone as he holds his daughter in his arms — dead from an assassin's bullet intended for him. It is at once a scream of dreadful hopelessness and pain, and his face contorts with terror and regret. He is lost and limp with sorrow, mouth wide open; but for twenty breathless seconds, there is no sound.

The riveting scene reminds me of the classic portrait *The Scream* by Edvard Munch, which depicts the isolation and the anonymity of anguish. It is art imitating life, and when first I saw it, I remember thinking, *I know the feeling.*

As in Coppola's *The Godfather* and Munch's *The Scream*, similar screams of faceless, nameless, marginalized minorities that have been discounted because of race, gender, religion, or nationality still cry out soundlessly. These are the ones victimized by the privilege and power inherited by dominant cultures or racial majorities that have evolved over time in both favor and fortune. Such silent screams only remind the impotent minority that perhaps the only thing worse than being a victim is being invisible.

I'm Just Asking

As with Michael Corleone, has this scream come too late? Are we hopelessly caught in a vicious cycle of violent retribution, human betrayal, and the quiet social genocide of racism? I'm just asking . . .

Should we, the free and the brave, accept and continue the status quo that allows certain people to enjoy special privileges based on the accident of birth? Do we dare confront the evil that rapes men and women of their dignity and molests their future because of their race or gender? I'm just asking . . .

Do we ourselves perpetuate the sin of racism by quietly practicing the advantages derived from being born to the right race in whichever nation we live? More specifically, have we rejected all remedies that do not simultaneously preserve advantage? And likewise, as in affirmative action, should we accept a remedy solely for purposes of redress, even though it creates additional innocent victims?

Can this national and generational curse that hangs around the necks of the offspring of both ex-slaves and ex-slave masters ever be rectified? Is there a viable institution suited to bring justice and reconciliation in the house? Who, if anyone, has the moral authority or jurisdiction, and where are they?

The Courts

In 1896, in the landmark case of *Plessy v. Fergusson*, the U.S. Supreme Court declared "separate but equal" constitutional, thereby legalizing segregation. In 1954, however, this same court, without including enforcement guidelines, reversed itself with *Brown v. Board of Education*.

Is there an alternative to turning to the highest court in the land to decide matters of such great weight? Where else might we look for answers? In a majority-rule democracy, who else could speak for the minority's rights? What about our moral institutions? What about the church?

The Church

In spite of its spotty record, I still believe the church is the best hope for a long-term solution to racism in America and perhaps around the world. However, the church must first overcome a serious credibility problem. Church splits have splintered the body, and denominations have created divisions based on race, doctrine, ideology, or nationality; so the problem becomes, which one or which part of the church is eligible or capable of preaching and practicing racial redemption?

Though she suffers her own "separate but equal" contradictions, despite her credibility issues, and because of her weak yet remaining ability to awaken the souls of men and women in ways courts and legislation cannot, the church remains our Hail Mary in these desperate days. Thankfully, a growing number of American churches across denominational lines are making great progress towards racial reconciliation. These churches represent microcosms of successful social revolution. What can we learn from the church communities that get it? How did they come to successfully celebrate the paradox of diversity *and* community?

Black in America

Being born black in America at times seems like a congenital defect. Unguided black children learn all too soon that their survival is uncertain; and faced with such uncertainty, they grow up selling their labor and loyalty to the lowest bidder.

Racism in America — or in any nation, for that matter; for it does exist in other parts of the world — is a conspicuous human tragedy lived daily by anonymous millions whose screams are seldom heard and whose stories are told only in the twisted sound bites and the bloody prose of a prejudiced prosecuting press that constantly blames the victim. It seems that no one knows their story, and no one cares.

They scream, and no one hears. They are faceless, voiceless, and invisible. They pray that someone, anyone, will notice. They long to be given a hearing by a just judge who will rule righteously and take into account the wicked variables that set them up to fail. They pray that someone will free them from the curse of being born in the right country but of the wrong race.

They become enraged at the unjust practices, the denials of opportunity and access, as they watch others who are younger and less prepared jump the line and steal their turn. Their parents tell them to be quiet, to wait for another turn, and not to cause trouble. "God sees," they say. It soon becomes apparent, however, that the cavalry is not coming; and if God sees, He must be a part of the conspiracy. All that's left to do, they conclude, is to extricate themselves and fight for their own freedom.

With this backdrop, it becomes evident that the broken black families and their scattered community must be reformed and restored. Leaders must emerge, or blacks in America will soon be relegated to a footnote in American history.

Stay with Me, Now — We're Going Somewhere

The chapters that follow represent the written screams of the disenfranchised, an emotional expression of both hurt and hope and an impassioned discussion of cause and effect. The following paragraphs and chapters are a sometimes politically incorrect eruption of raw feelings and, therefore, need ongoing forgiveness as this book fights for a redemptive conclusion. And, by the way, in spite of itself, it does end in redemption.

This is not a deep discussion. My point is not to be clever, but clear. My words represent the passionate musings of a Detroit "projects boy" who loves America and who was taught to love everybody unconditionally, regardless of race, religion, or nationality, but who found that hard to do in the face of the blatant racism in religion and society that crippled his kind. These musings are a blend of history, both religious and political, and attempt to identify, expose, and exorcise the demons that divide us — the greatest of which is racism.

In these few pages, I add yet another voice to the chorus. Common threads run throughout each chapter, like a chorus that repeats after each verse of a song. I have tried to define our times in real-world terms and update the consciences of believers who have laid down their swords and now stand with only a shield. I aim to hold accountable those who claim the name of Christ —

for their actions or inaction, for their vote or refusal to vote that passively aids and abets the dark forces of power politics that overwhelm our good sense and, if possible, would even undermine our faith.

In the end, I want to lead us to the principal issue as well as a principled solution. This treatise exposes a demonic nemesis to humankind that I call the spirit of division. Racism is perhaps the leading manifestation of this spirit, although not the only one. Equally devastating and following close on its heels is denominationalism.

Denominationalism is the church's racism. It is the primary reason that churches have little moral authority. Religion and racism are inextricably related and operate with similar and simultaneous histories and equal dysfunction, which demands that we look at them both as we search for cause, effect, and solution. Fix these two, denominationalism and racism, and sexism and classism have no cover. If the mighty force that we call the kingdom of God, which includes the universal church, is going to not only make a difference but also win new converts, it must first correct itself; and the time to do it is now.

God of Our Weary Years is essentially a spiritual inside look from a black perspective at the pain and disease of racism and how it can be defeated by unrelenting and unconditional love. It walks us through the dark realities while leading to the bright possibilities of interracial and ecumenical community.

But in order to get there, we must first face our fear, ignorance, arrogance, denial, pain, and shame. We must review the histories we think we already know. We must embrace and respect every perspective, no matter how provoking and self-serving they appear to be. Getting at the truth of who we were, who we are, and who we are destined to become must be paramount.

Joe Hopkins, a close friend of mine who is a prominent civil rights attorney and publisher of the *Journal* newspaper in Pasadena, California, made an interesting statement in citing the transformation of the controversial Malcolm X. In his book *I Will Not Apologize*, Hopkins says, "Personal growth comes from seeking and finding truth, not ignoring it. Malcolm learned by listening first to his elders in his chosen religion — Islam. He learned more when he went to Mecca to find truth for himself. He didn't reject the truth of what he saw in Mecca. He instead realized that some people of all colors and races are good and some are bad."

Regardless of your personal opinions concerning Malcolm X, the powerful point of the transformative nature of truth and self-discovery must not be lost in all the controversial rhetoric. As you wrestle with the demons inherent to the journey, a transformation just as deep as the one Malcolm X experienced can be yours — if you are willing to embrace the truth.

I urge you to be challenged by my sometimes politically incorrect language and the unsparing rhetoric of an urban warrior. Regardless of your race, look not away from the ugly truth of my experiences and those of millions like me. Look at me and believe what I tell you, without the self-serving defense that is the luxury of the powerful and the privileged.

At the risk of your outright rejection, I have chosen not to make diplomacy my goal, lest you miss the point, which, for the purposes of this book, seems best made by plain talk. When you feel your first twinge of anger, I beg you to keep reading. If you feel like smiling or even laughing because something strikes you as humorous or even off-beat, seize the opportunity while you can, but keep reading. My bet is that your senses and empathy will be awakened as you read and reason with me. I further wager that the investment of patience will pay off in the end. Please remember that this is written from a black perspective, for I know no other. I pray that my love for you will shield you from any offense you may take. I assure you, none is intended.

Discussion Guide

At the end of each chapter, I have provided four questions designed to stimulate interaction and provoke further thought and discussion in church, school, or university classrooms. It is my hope that *God of Our Weary Years* will inspire dialogue among diverse groups and perhaps lead to twenty-first-century solutions to the age-old problem of racial and religious divisions.

PART 1

THE SPIRIT OF DIVISION:
Where Racism Finds Its Roots

Chapter 1

THE SPLIT SCREEN

It was October 3, 1995, ten o' clock in the morning. Low clouds had lifted, revealing a blue autumn sky over the lush green San Gabriel Mountains. We were only minutes away from the announcement of the verdict of the century. This is not just exciting—this is historical, I thought, as I hastily moved to my family room to turn on the larger of the television sets and to call my brother in Detroit with whom I always shared significant current events.

It was an incredible moment. My heart pounded as my sweaty hands dialed Roland's home phone. I wondered aloud whether the verdict would emancipate, vindicate, or merely verify just how stuck we were. My pessimism anticipated the latter. No matter the decision, we knew we had approached a tipping point in the United States of America.

Separated by geography but united by a phone line and the special love that brothers share, Roland and

I dropped our prognostications and listened intently as CNN zeroed in on the fifty-one-year-old jury forewoman. "Okay, okay, here we go," Roland whispered.

"We, the jury, in the above entitled action, find the defendant, James Orenthal Simpson, not guilty of the crime of murder."

Roland and I began to yell and scream, just as if Michigan had just defeated Ohio State. My family room was filled with jubilant shouts of "Yes! Yes! Yes!" followed by "Oh God!" and "Thank You, Lord!" Above the din of noise in my family room, I heard my brother say, "I love you, boy!" I answered, "I love you too. I gotta go."

As I put the phone down, CNN split the viewing screen and progressed from showing the scene in front of the courthouse to pictures of reactions around the country. Like the air going out of a balloon, my joy quickly subsided. It was like a storm cloud that comes rolling in to obscure a previously sunny day. In a matter of seconds, great sadness slowly replaced the great elation in my heart. I stood transfixed as I witnessed on that split television screen the division in America. In every case, black Americans wildly rejoiced, but white Americans stood stunned, silent, and horrified, with a "what just happened" look on their faces.

I remember thinking, with obvious understatement, *This is not going to be good, and it "ain't" over!* I ran out of the room, ignoring the ringing phone. I headed over to our local pastors' monthly reconciliation meeting.

A House Divided

Arriving at the meeting location, I instinctively knew this session could not be business as usual. That very day, Dr. John Perkins was handing over leadership to me in preparation for his move back to Mississippi. After politely greeting one another, I noted that we were all standing in racially separated groups. The black pastors were buzzing about the verdict in one corner of the room, while the white pastors mingled in subdued and quiet conversation. Gradually we drifted together in polite greetings and small talk, feebly attempting to divert our attention from the inevitable discussion and waiting patiently for the chair's meeting-called-to-order announcement.

I had whispered to John that we might need to drop the agenda and deal with the obvious disparity of feelings over the news of the day. John agreed, and in his masterful way, the man considered the father of reconciliation in America and a prolific author on the subject led the prayer of invocation, which included a prayer for God's healing and peace.

John's prayer was profound and penetrating. An eerie and quiet reverence settled over the room. Another voice continued the prayer: "Father, help us now to live out the unconditional love we talk about." I could not discern whose voice it was, but I knew it was one of the white pastors. We all seemed to sense that this was a moment of truth. Were we serious about our pledge to be a Christian community? Was the reconciliation we talked about merely religious rhetoric, or did we, in truth, value racial identity above Christian unity?

As I pondered these questions, I wondered what could possibly bridge this latest breach. I was sure it was primarily a breach in perception. We each viewed the same incident from very different worlds. It became clear to me that the first step and the first battle must be fought here: understanding, accepting, then overcoming perceptions.

Personally, how did I feel? I was at once both glad and sad. The Simpson verdict in some way made it feel as though the injustice of the Rodney King verdict was rectified. *Now they know how we felt*, I thought, as I tried unsuccessfully to justify my joy and conveniently ignored my them-versus-us attitude. Yet something in me was torturing my senses and somehow implying that my pride was out of order.

The incongruence between my heart and my head awakened a war between my feelings and my faith. For the first time in my life, I had a feeling that did not reconcile with my faith. John stretched out his arms, and the men on each side of him grabbed his hands. Instinctively everyone else followed until there was a circle around the room and every hand was being held. It was apparent that this pastors' meeting was turning into a prayer meeting.

I really did not want to spiritualize this moment. I wanted to celebrate. I wanted to savor this moment of victory as if it were some long overdue payback. I had met a new monster that was actually quite old, and he was in me—vengeance. I was consumed with a spirit of vengeance. Two people had been viciously murdered. The accused was acquitted, and all over the world, blacks were glad and whites were mad. On this day, I just wanted to celebrate being black and being on the winning side—nothing else. But this other thing was in the room, competing for my moment.

The prevailing wind of prayer ushered in a powerful spirit of peace and a mysterious yet compelling need to stay right there. I sensed the Holy Spirit whispering, "Don't speak while I am speaking; don't move while I am moving." Maybe I was the only one who could hear that voice. Perhaps I was the only one who needed to hear it. I had chosen vengeance over forgiveness, anger over love, and justice over peace—so much for my "Christian witness."

How did I get here? How long have I been here? How will I ever be free from these conflicting feelings? Who says I should be free? These and a thousand other thoughts raced through my mind. The battle between human reason and my kingdom-of-God training raged within me. I knew the rules. How could peace ever come if I demanded payment for past injustice? This was not the message of reconciliation of 2 Corinthians 5:19.

My silent argument continued: *This jury's verdict is at least as good as the all-white jury that acquitted the four white policemen who beat Rodney King sober, isn't it? . . . Why do white people always think they are right and everybody else is wrong? . . . Why should I repent? . . . For what should I repent?*

No sooner had I thought the last question than the answer came: vengeance. I was indiscriminately and indiscreetly vengeful. In fact, I could go one better and say that revenge was what I wanted. How about that? Man, I was on a roll! My spirit was foul and out of control—yet I celebrated. I lost complete sight of my principal Christian beliefs. Revenge, vengeance, payback—yes! That is what my wounded heart longed for. Vengeance, I knew, belonged to God. I knew it, but I didn't care. I didn't care because nobody had ever cared about us. On that fateful day, I wanted justice—not peace.

I had never experienced this feeling before. For the first time, I realized that for years I had taken refuge in being a victim. Over time, I had embraced the self-righteous arrogance that broods and breeds in the victims of racism. I felt entitled to it, and today was payday. It seemed a hellish paradox. Justice and forgiveness were in hand-to-hand combat. I didn't want to choose sides—not today.

At that very moment, the sound of another man praying made its way to my ears. "Oh God," he cried, "forgive me for my blindness; forgive me for my stupidity. Please, Father, forgive me for being so insensitive. Bind our hearts together through this experience; please help this group to make a difference."

I was stunned by the heartfelt cry emanating from this man's lips. I turned to see who was raining on my parade and saw that it was one of our leading white pastors. I reached for him, and as we embraced, I whispered my own confession: "I'm so sorry. Please forgive me. I'm so sorry." My words were involuntary; something within me pushed them out. Mercifully, I was not alone. The wind of the Spirit of God swept through the room. It was a spontaneous and corporate outpouring, a genuine baptism of love that led to an equally genuine baptism of repentance.

That moment refreshed in each of us the desire to listen, to trust, and to reconcile at a totally new level — a level without precondition. The only question remaining was, would we be able to leverage this supernatural moment into a lasting ministry of racial reconciliation within our community? Where should we go from here? This was, indeed, a new level and just maybe a new beginning.

John Perkins, a godly man, reminded me of my father. His forehead was creased with two permanent wrinkles, and his dark skin bore the marks of his unique experience of being beaten and jailed in Mississippi. Remarkably, he had come out on the other side of his experience with a fierce dedication to racial reconciliation. In the hood, we would say, he had "street creds," and that morning they stood him tall as he refused to allow us to miss the opportunity to practice what we preached.

With a moral authority earned in the damp hell of more than one Mississippi jail, he commanded us to submit our personal feelings to the greater goal: the unity of the community and the kingdom of God. The questions that faced us were not limited to personal bias, racial pride, sense of justice, or raw emotion, but rather addressed the broader questions of what the church's position should be and how best to advance a kingdom-of-God agenda during this tumultuous time.

John preached about biblical reconciliation with a power and authority that united every heart in the building, at least for that moment. We were challenged to come forward and commit ourselves at the altar, and many responded. In that session, we agreed to later convene a citywide unity meeting for area churches at the great Lake Avenue Congregational Church in Pasadena.

I was asked to give closing remarks and a benediction. I addressed the audience of almost two thousand from the compelling perspective of most black Americans (the flesh dies slowly). I wanted the whites to understand what blacks were thinking and feeling — that their silent screams had been given voice in a verdict. I needed all sides to be held accountable for the minority view. I felt I could not allow the pain of black Americans to again be submerged in religious guilt and the sheer weight of majority opinion. I stubbornly sought to weave an ethnocentric rationale into the powerful Christ-centered message spoken by Dr. Perkins just minutes earlier.

I forged ahead. As best I could, I explained that for blacks it was not primarily about the guilt or innocence of O. J. Simpson or the tragic murders. For us, the verdict was symbolic of the fairness and justice that we had so long been denied. It provided a sense of vindication — the kind that comes when you (blacks) are finally in the majority (the jury) and use the power of majority rule to prevent the conviction of a man who, from your perspective, may have been set up by the police. In some inexplicable way, it seemed to make up for the countless others who had been victimized and wrongly convicted by a society that determined their merit and their guilt or innocense based on the color of their skin.

As a man of God, I did follow this by publicly apologizing for momentarily laying aside all thoughts of racial reconciliation in favor of celebrating. I repented for putting my feelings above the purposes of the kingdom of God. There — it was off my chest; I got it said. I prayed a short benediction prayer and left the stage, but I was not prepared for what followed.

As I descended from the platform, white men and women, both old and young, rushed me. Some fell on my shoulder and tearfully repented to me for not understanding the pain of the African American past that I had apparently represented in my benediction speech. An expression of pain coupled with an act of love born in repentance had begotten other acts of love and repentance. I was humbled. I felt unworthy. My deliverance had begun.

Grace and Mercy

Clearly, God's agenda preempts personal agendas, no matter how heartfelt and justifiable they may be. The eternal strategy for evangelizing the world always takes precedence and priority over all earthly events and often includes a cross to be borne before a crown can be worn. That strategy of love and unity is the greatest mandate in Scripture, and it was prayed for by none other than Jesus Himself:

> I'm praying not only for them but also for those who will believe in me because of them and their witness about me. The goal is for all of them to become one heart and mind—just as you, Father, are in me and I in you, so they might be one heart and mind with us. Then the world might believe that you, in fact, sent me. The same glory you gave me, I gave them, so they'll be unified and together as we are—I in them and you in me. Then they'll be mature in this oneness, and give the godless world evidence that you've sent me and loved them in the same way you've loved me.
>
> —John 17:20–23 MSG

In our struggle for community in the context of race, we must have the courage to take a hard look at ourselves, our beliefs, and our systems for living out those beliefs. The talk is far easier than the walk, I will admit. But it is absolutely imperative that we sit at each other's feet, learn of each other's journey, and appreciate and tolerate the feelings and ideas from across the track so that we might celebrate our diversity as opposed to using that diversity to determine privilege and advantage.

It is equally clear that the key to unlocking the chains of racism lies in the hands of the victims of racism. They are the ones with the moral authority and perhaps the moral obligation to set free those who have consciously or unconsciously perpetrated and perpetuated this terrible sin upon powerless masses. We who call ourselves victims must declare peace and refuse to exact payback. We who have received by grace the forgiveness of our trespasses must drop all claims against those who have trespassed against us.

The victims of racism and racial discrimination must break the power of generational curses by extravagantly and publicly renouncing all rights, both real and imagined, to justice and retribution as a remedy for their ills. In order for their sacrifice to dispel the darkness even more, they must lavishly celebrate the return home of racial prodigals, both black and white: blacks, from their wars of revolution; and whites, from their wars of preservation.

Keep It Real

I believe that the power of unconditional love can and will break down every barrier built by racism, bigotry, and discrimination of all kinds. Over time, stubborn love will cast out these ageless demons of humanity. The bridge that will unite the great divide is called grace and mercy, but it cannot be built or crossed without great sacrifice from all the stakeholders.

The greatest sacrifice any member of a majority race can make is the sacrifice of time—time to listen, learn, understand, and enter into the myriad of foul experiences of minorities that resulted in the pathologies that have marked, scarred, and limited so many for so long. Likewise, the greatest sacrifice that can be made by blacks is the giving up of a sometimes preoccupation with redress, along with the accompanying self-righteous and self-destructive anger to which we have been devoted for the past sixty years.

Many blacks, however, are still angry and venting from the memory of violent incidents that never received the closure that justice and restitution bring. Trapped by color, our bitterness, anger, hatred, and perception of being a permanent underclass make it difficult, if not impossible, for us to have a calm discussion about race without losing control and lashing out with the vitriol of pent-up feelings. We can be in a room with people sympathetic to our position yet still find it difficult not to command the floor and demand attention be given to "what you did to us."

I was in such a meeting several years ago with seven or eight other pastors. Black, white, and Hispanic, we were seeking ways to serve the community and share resources. When the white leader of the "rich white church" suggested that too many black churches were wasting resources by doing the same ministry, I exploded. My premise was that his suggestion disrespected the years of service of the black pastors in the room and ignored their long and close relationships which in the black community is honored over resources; besides, neither he nor the majority of members of his church lived in the city.

I was on my feet and mad. My anger was unhidden and unbridled. When the smoke settled, the young son of my spiritual father, John Perkins, spoke up. Derrick had been through a few racial-reconciliation confrontations and apparently had seen this picture before. Looking at the red-faced pastor to whom my remarks were directed, this young African American said, "Forgive Pastor Cushman; he's still venting."

Until that moment, I had never thought of myself as venting. I immediately became defensive and pointed to the facts of the matter. But no one came to my rescue. My tone and spirit had overridden my intent. My "truth" was lost in the vomit of my sickness. My anger had been stalking my reason for a long time.

It took this very tense and risky moment to expose to me the vulnerable underbelly of hope. Underneath our efforts to love is the vitally important need to be understood and to understand where the feelings come from. While unconditional, stubborn, thick-skinned love is the only thing that can bridge the great racial divide, I also believe that equal to the power of love is the power of understanding. "With all thy getting get understanding" (Prov. 4:7 KJV).

If love does not include understanding, it is reduced to a ceremonial exercise in futility, much like the fifth-Sunday unity meetings my denomination celebrated, where we convinced ourselves we were actually bringing the races together. Such meetings, however, became substitutes for real dialogue with the real and intentional purpose of unifying and reconciling people who carried real hurts. They never dealt with the root causes and effects of our disunity. But to eradicate the root causes, we must at least try to understand their origins and applications.

The prerequisite for understanding any social group, especially those of a different culture and race, is dialogue. We must tell each other our stories from our different points of view. We must listen patiently as hurt people vent both their sorrow and their rage. We must hear "the enemy" (whether red, yellow, black, white, or brown) speak from his or her perspective. We must sit on our hands and bite our lips and our tongues until they bleed, if necessary. We must do whatever we have to do—but we must listen. Love partnered with understanding is the antidote that attacks the problem at its root.

Discussion Guide

1. In what ways was the O. J. Simpson verdict a bellwether for race relations in the United States? What were your own reactions to the verdict?

2. What questions would you ask or what statements would you make if you were a participant in a racial-reconciliation study group?

3. What were your feelings immediately following the Rodney King verdict of 1992? From your perspective, describe what made this verdict just or unjust. How are the O. J. Simpson verdict and the Rodney King verdict similar, and how are they different?

4. How important is it to understand a person's history? Identify at least three ways in which we can diffuse the generational anger of victims of racism.

Chapter 2

IN THE BEGINNING

Stuff Happens

Even though I have grown to like the idea of the separation of church and state, I have begun to believe that the separation of church and state may be the proverbial oxymoron—possible and impossible at the same time. It may be desirable but not realistic. Of course, my premise begins from a truly creationist proposition.

If God created man in His own image and predestined him from before the foundation of the world to carry out His divine purpose, then separating man from Him is like separating a newborn from its mother, separating the object from its source. Church, therefore, goes with state, much like hand goes with glove, and wet goes with water. Man lives, moves, and has manifestation in the state.

My Christian perspective further holds that man's success in the earth, or in the state, is in direct proportion to his acknowledgment and inclusion of God. And because of the compelling connection of the divine with humankind, man consciously and subconsciously seeks to scratch the itch caused by the greatest love he has ever known — the love of God. God has determined to love us and has made it all but impossible to be utterly and finally separated from Him. So determined is the Creator to love the creature and to be loved by His creation, He devised a remedy for the separation before the separation ever occurred.

Before the fall of man, there already existed a strategy for recovery. From before the foundation of the world — even before we were ever created — there was a fail-safe rescue plan. So wrestle with this phenomenal thought: the Spirit of division that came into the world at the time of man's fall has already been defeated in God's eternal strategy.

The seeds of racism, classism, sexism, and all forms of human division were sown in the sin of Adam and Eve. The genders divided as Eve stepped outside of Adam's covering, and Adam, in turn, blamed Eve for the disobedience that divided them from God. The family divided when Cain killed Abel because of jealousy, and so the die of division was cast. It has since morphed into even greater evil divisions where the latter is always more corrupt than the former, but with all violating the prerequisite principles of unity, synergy, and agreement established between God and His creation.

The battle between the spirit of unity and the spirit of division is symptomatic of the greater war between

God and Satan, or good and evil. The lines have been drawn since creation. Humankind, the crown of God's creation, is the domain over which the battle is fought. Satan's primary strategy in this battle is to conquer the kingdom by dividing the subjects through any means possible.

In his evil plan, he divides men and women from God and from each other, just as he did with the first couple in the garden of Eden. He still divides families, just as he did with Cain and Abel, or Noah and his sons. He still tempts men to covet power without covenant, such as what happened in the building of the Tower of Babel. Because of humankind's effort to gain unbridled power, God confused their language and scattered them all over the earth: "So the Lord scattered them from there over all the earth, and they stopped building the city" (Gen. 11:8).

The evil one also divides nations, as he did between the offspring of Sarah and Hagar, between Israel and Judah, and between Jew and Gentile. He divides the children of God into many religions: Islam, Judaism, Christianity, Buddhism, Hinduism, and myriad others. But perhaps the most powerful of all these divisions perpetuated by this prince of darkness is racism, accompanied by its evil cousins ethnic cleansing, religious genocide, and racial homicide.

However, from the very beginning, even in the Old Testament, God cursed racism when it raised its ugly head. When Miriam uttered her bigoted response about her brother Moses' Cushite wife, a black woman from the land of Cush (modern-day Ethiopia), God struck her with leprosy. Note that the Bible clearly states that it was the Lord—not Moses—who heard and reacted to the slur against Moses' Cushite wife.

The implication of the passage is that Moses, said to be more humble than anyone on the face of the earth, did not hear the slur and may not have done anything about it if he had. However, the all-hearing ear of God did hear it, and God moved against Miriam drastically and immediately. Were it not for the passionate plea of her brother Moses interceding on her behalf, she may well have died in that condition.

By the time Jesus was born in a Bethlehem manger one starry night, his family tree looked like a multicultural rainbow of races, including no less than the blood of Rahab the harlot (Matt. 1:5). Can you imagine the DNA of a harlot coexisting with the DNA of the all-holy Jehovah God? But that is exactly what happened!

Indeed, this was an undeniable prophetic act of restoration principled in the old covenant (Old Testament) and perfected in the new covenant (New Testament). And the clinching verse relative to race that summarizes the mind and intent of God from the very beginning is found in the new covenant, Jesus' last will and testament. Acts 17:26 spells it out clearly: "And hath made of one blood all nations of men for to dwell on all the face of the earth, and hath determined the times before appointed, and the bounds of their habitations" (KJV).

So, what is *our* problem? Our problem is congenital. We are born in sin — all of us. It is the classic battle waged between flesh and spirit. It is the very nature of sin that causes mankind to make choices against his own best interest. Racism is a self-destructive human evil that attempts to preserve the part at the expense of the whole. It is *I* versus *we*. It results in a them-versus-us existence of those God "hath made of one blood all nations of men."

It is evident that racism is the result of Adam's fall, and all of us are infected and affected by the resulting diseases. Racism is a primary manifestation of the spirit of the evil one and expresses itself as the invention of depraved, unredeemed humanity seeking what Adam and Eve sought in their fateful failure in the garden: to gain advantage over creation for themselves. They fell for the seductive suggestion of the evil one: "You shall not surely die: For God doth know that in the day ye eat thereof, then your eyes shall be opened, and ye shall be as gods, knowing good and evil" (Gen. 3:4–5 KJV).

The suggestion is, if I am as God, I won't need God. The lust for power, privilege, and advantage that has the potential to establish and perpetuate one's self or even itself originates in the original-sin condition. Self-reliance, at first glance, seems noble, but when it means independence from the Creator, our life-giver and our source, it is always the beginning of the end.

We live in a humanistic postmodern era where human beings have declared relationship and dependence on God to be the opiate of the ignorant and unlearned. We have been seduced by the tantalizing possibilities of going it alone, having the power to do our own thing and suppressing or oppressing any group or individual different from our own.

In the beginning, there was chaos. Jehovah God spoke to Himself and said, "Let us . . ." — and there was. Chaos immediately gave way to order, and time began to follow a blueprint written in eternity that included the plan and purpose for humankind. It was in eternity that God prepared the answer to every question in time. It was in eternity that the omnipotent God set in motion laws to govern both the heavens and the hamlets in the realm of time. It was in eternity that the omniscient God anticipated and planned the response to every variable resulting from man's exercise of free will.

God's perfectly balanced response would enable His kingdom to come and His will to eventually be done on earth — perfectly — as it is in heaven. Before time began the omnipresent God brought order to the chaos, light to the darkness, and a solution to every problem everywhere at every time in history. With His own death and resurrection, He guaranteed the restoration of His beloved and brought balance to the eternal equation.

From Chicago to Shanghai and from Nairobi to Nome — red, yellow, black, and white — we, you and I, are His beloved. He decorated the earth with human diversity, and one day He will reintroduce us to eternity where we will finally see Him as He is and know Him and one another as we are known. No longer will we see through the tinted glass of our earthly flesh, but finally we will know one another completely.

Until then we must learn what He already knows about us. He knew that the crown of His creation would be accosted by the demon spirit of division and all its subgroups. Yet He showed us the design, assured us of His eternal love and commitment, gave us His own Spirit, and promised us we would win in the end, no matter what it looks like now. Racism and denominationalism have been nailed to the cross, and in Him their defeat and our restoration are complete.

It is often said that knowing is half the battle, and I agree with that. Knowing this great plan of God's enables me to deal with the many human manifestations of the fall and the fallout from original sin. Knowledge of God's great comprehensive strategy is half the battle to defeat racism and denominationalism. Winning begins with knowing, and God knows. "For whom he did foreknow he also did predestinate to be conformed to the image of his Son, that he might be the firstborn among many brethren. Moreover whom he did predestinate, them he also called: and whom he called, them he also justified: and whom he justified, them he also glorified" (Rom. 8:29–30 KJV).

Discussion Guide

1. Discuss the limitations of the separation of church and state. What all does this principle affect?

2. What, in your opinion, are the key divisions in American society? Relate them to the spirit of division in our world.

3. What do Rahab and Jesus have in common? What is the principle, the political and the racial lesson, learned from the story of the biblical story of Rahab?

4. How does the knowledge of God's foreknowledge make a difference in your perspective of racism and denominationalism?

Chapter 3

DAMAGED DNA

Rulership by way of genetic dynasty was not the plan of God and has proven to be perhaps man's greatest curse since his fall in the garden of Eden. Hereditary privilege is a postcreation evil symptomatic of the fall of man from a far superior grace. Man was created in the image of God and as such enjoyed the highest status of all created things. He started at the top. He could never inherit greater power, privilege, or position than what he received in the beginning.

There was only one direction for man to go—down. Thus we refer to the proximal changes after his creation as "the fall." Consequently, everything after man's fall from grace was inferior to his original status. The original covenant, government, health plan, labor relations, family order, and social order were all superior to what followed after man's decision to disobey God.

Everything that God created was originally part of a complex tapestry. The universe is held together through the confluence of Divine Providence and the laws of nature set in motion by that Divine Providence. Out of this confluence flows a perfect harmony — a balanced equation of diverse creatures and species of creatures with varied and specific purposes. It is majestically ordered by a covenant instinctive to the entire universe, animate and inanimate, with the exception of one.

God's last act of bringing order out of chaos was to crown His creation with the human race. "And God said, Let us make man in our image, after our likeness: and let them have dominion over the fish of the sea, and over the fowl of the air, and over the cattle, and over all the earth, and over every creeping thing that creepeth upon the earth. So God created man in his own image, in the image of God created he him; male and female created he them" (Gen. 1:26–27 KJV).

Man was distinguished from all other creatures by two things: the gift of free will and his possession of God's likeness: "So God created man in his own image, in the image of God created he him." My pastor, Rick Hawkins, often says, "God's first idea is His final decision." Here is the point: He made only one race of people. He reminded us again several thousand years later that this was intentional. He has not changed the facts of the story. "God that made the world and all things therein, seeing that he is Lord of heaven and earth, dwelleth not in temples made with hands; neither is worshipped with men's hands, as though he needed any thing; seeing he giveth to all life, and breath, and all things; and *hath made of one blood all nations of men* for to dwell on all the face of the earth, and hath determined the times before appointed, and the bounds of their habitation" (Acts 17:24–26 KJV, emphasis added).

There is no super race. Even the Jews are not a special race. They were not created out of the ground or from thin air after Adam and Eve sinned. They were simply carved out of Gentiles who agreed to join God in a sacred covenant. It is important to remember that it was an act of faith and obedience that brought them into covenant relationship. They are Jews because of this covenant; they don't have covenant because they are Jews. They are Jews because they are special; they are not special because they are Jews.

The specific purpose of the Jews was to be the conduit through which God in the flesh would be born. By the time Jesus was born of the Virgin Mary in Bethlehem, almost every race was represented in His bloodline—the good, the bad, and the ugly. Rahab the harlot, whose story is recorded in Joshua 6:17–25, is also listed in Jesus' family tree recorded in Matthew 1:5.

Clearly, the creation of the Jews was not about bloodline or race—it was about covenant. The all-wise and all-knowing God knew that the evil one would attempt to rob Him of some, if not all, of the crown jewels of His creation. Through the corrupting of man's reason and the resulting rise of adversarial races, cultures, and kingdoms, the enemy launched his attack to divide and conquer. God, therefore, wisely included various races and nationalities in Jesus' genealogy and genetic composition. While I am proud to be part of that royal lineage, I cannot stake claim to the whole — not that it matters. So who then is a true Jew?

Who Is a Jew?

According to Romans 2:28, the sign of covenant has changed. In the New Testament, God elevates the symbol of covenant from physical to spiritual, thus fulfilling His original intent that "in thee [Abraham] shall *all* families of the earth be blessed" (Gen. 12:3 KJV, emphasis added). God's natural progressions are always from imperfect to perfect; thus, our restoration will not be complete until the imperfect gives way to the perfect. Under the old covenant, the physical circumcision of the male was the mark of covenant. But in the new covenant, it is the spiritual circumcision of the heart in both male and female, Jew and non-Jew, slave and free. God has "made of one blood *all* nations of men for to dwell on all the face of the earth" (Acts 17:26 KJV, emphasis added).

Principled in creation is family. Unique to family is the paradox of unity amid diversity. From the day Cain killed Abel, all the peoples of the earth have been afflicted by the curse of division, which produced family, clan, tribal, and national rivalries. The curse existed not in the plan, but in the people who had to walk out the plan. However, the omniscient God, knowing that man was corrupted by sin, anticipated every breakdown, failure, and departure from divine destiny and prepared for it in advance.

The Jews were God's model family; consequently, they prophetically modeled the relationship between

God and His children. When we view this relationship under the Old Testament (old covenant), we get a preview of the Father's intention and purpose for each of us today under the New Testament (new covenant). While the Jews had a purpose different from the nations around them, it must be noted that historically *whoever* worshiped and obeyed God enjoyed His favor. This was true because the basis for relationship with God is faith and obedience — not race, religion, or nationality.

Historically God had mercy on nonbelieving nations when they believed and obeyed. The non-Jewish Ninevites heeded Jonah's warning of impending destruction, and God had mercy on them. Providential alliance caused Ruth, a young Moabite woman, to become one of the ancestors of Christ, and that same purpose-driven providence caused Esther, a Jewess, to marry a Gentile king and consequently preserve Israel.

Though humanity fractured into families, tribes, clans, races, and nations, God never redefined His divine purpose: that man would glorify Him in his diversity and that all humanity had been created from one blood in the beginning and would be redeemed by one blood in the end.

Even though Israel consisted of twelve tribes with ongoing civil feuds, the beginning of the end of their favored-nation status came when they decided they wanted a king, like the other nations. "Nevertheless the people refused to obey the voice of Samuel; and they said, Nay; but we will have a king over us; that we also may be like all the nations; and that our king may judge us, and go out before us, and fight our battles. . . . And the Lord said to Samuel, Hearken unto their voice, and make them a king" (1 Sam. 8:19–20, 22 KJV).

What is significant about this give-us-a-king demand is that it marks the beginning of a new governing paradigm called "the kingdom age," and it represents man's second major attempt at independence. The first attempt included an outside tempter, the serpent, who suggested to Eve in the garden, "Ye shall not surely die: For God doth know that in the day ye eat thereof, then your eyes shall be opened, and ye shall be as gods, knowing good and evil" (Gen. 3:4–5 KJV).

In the second attempt at independence, the demand for a king, we see the same desire to live independently of God. This carryover of the Edenic curse set off another chain reaction of division and death, just like the first act of disobedience had done. Disobedience always brings death to relationships, whether between God and man, family members, friends, or business partners.

A covenant is an agreement between two parties. When the agreement is broken, the relationship suffers and sometimes dies, the advocates become adversaries, and the parties are separated by the breach of contract. If the breach is not bridged and the relationship is not reconciled, the separated parties become combatants, competitors, and, in the end, enemies.

The chain reaction of division and death went from God and man, to Cain and Abel, to Ishmael and Isaac, to

Esau and Jacob, to Joseph and his brothers, and to David and his brothers. In each case, the division unleashed a chain reaction of generational feuding, fighting, and fracturing into warring factions and nations.

Discussion Guide

1. Identify the genetic dynasties of the twenty-first century.

2. Who is the model family of the Old Testament? Who is the model family of the New Testament?

3. In the kingdom age, do you think that the literal Jews are God's chosen people? Why or why not?

4. What privileges did you inherit at birth? When you were born again, what privileges did you gain?

Chapter 4

THE PHENOMENON OF MAJORITY

The American Heritage Dictionary, Second College Edition, defines the word *majority* as "the greater number or part; a number that is more than half of the whole; a number that when reached grants rights and privilege, as in the 'age of majority.' " *Majority rule* is defined as "a political doctrine by which a numerical majority of the voters holds the power to make decisions binding on all the voters." Let's look at both of these definitions in greater detail and see how they relate to the topic at hand.

Majority Rule: Peril and Paradox

From the biblical perspective, we have acknowledged that racism and other forms of division ultimately find their origins in the garden of Eden. From that same perspective, when we go back to the beginning, what we also learn is that sin separates.   However,

Chapter 4 • The Phenomenon of Majority   35

racism's strength and ability to perpetuate itself is also rooted in a very natural phenomenon: numerical and political majorities.

Majorities have ruled since time began, and societies operate by the majority's rules. Being born a member of a majority can be a significant asset as one finds his or her way in the world. Majorities determine identity, privilege, and advantage for themselves and even determine the identities of minorities. Majorities write the books considered, by them at least, "official," and whether truth or fiction, these books not only chronicle the majority's own history but also chronicle, minimize, and in some cases totally eliminate the histories of minorities.

Majorities not only determine but also define. The terms that govern, the prevailing values, and the priorities of the overall social construct are defined by the majority. Majorities perpetuate themselves by leaving legacies that empower their kind for generations. Power majorities determine privilege, such as who gets to vote, who gets the best opportunities, who gets the best education, who can borrow money, and who can live where.

Interestingly, numerical majority alone does not guarantee power. For example, the South African apartheid, which was arguably the worse form of racism in the world, was perpetrated by a numerical minority that enjoyed a power majority. Numerically, in the population as a whole, the whites of South Africa were outnumbered seven to one; but because they were the numerical majority in government, in the military, and in commerce, they were able to control and perpetuate the impotence of the numerical majority, the native black African. Through the ruthless tyranny of fear, deprivation, and subjugation, this power majority managed to retain control.

Before apartheid ended in 1994, Cuban communists had already begun to infiltrate South Africa with plans to liberate it, as they had done in Angola. Indeed, it was only by divine intervention brought on by the invasion of the kingdom of God that a nationwide bloodbath was prevented. The kingdom of God sent in wave after wave of intercessory prayer warriors, followed by a relentless bombardment of the word of reconciliation. The siege of racism was broken as men and women of God, such as Bishop Desmond Tutu, Bishop Joseph Garlington, Dr. Samuel J. Hines, the intercessory prayer teams supporting them, and other spiritual agents fighting behind enemy lines, caused the sudden and miraculous release of Nelson Mandela. While Mandela's release was not seen as a spiritual event by the church, it was, nonetheless, the result of spiritual warfare. In spite of his lack of notable religious affiliation, his release was a direct answer to prayer and served a purpose greater than Mandela himself.

Mandela's release sent the white minority government into retreat under the increasingly heavy and daily burden of world opinion. A chain reaction of events and pressure exerted by student activists around the world, combined with the sanctions urged by groups like TransAfrica led by Randall Robinson, resulted in the pullout of major business corporations and signaled the defeat of apartheid as an official policy.

Certainly, that stronghold has not been completely broken, and unless South Africa comes to God, it will not be able to eradicate an even more powerful racism: tribal division and rivalry. South Africa and its neighbor Namibia must replace their idolatrous worship of ancestral tradition with the principles of God's Word, or they face simply exchanging the evils of apartheid for the chaos of tribal conflict. Or even worse, they may reap the legacy of apartheid in a new form, with the demons of racism returning seven times stronger in the form of black-on-black ethnic cleansing.

Furthermore, although the black African numerical majority is ruling politically, a white power majority is still ruling the economy. If hearts and minds are not changed, this can easily become the corridor for a racist insurgency that rules from behind the scenes. The only thing that will prevent the continuation of racism in that country or any other country is the preeminence of kingdom rules where God's subjects exercise dominion according to His Word, which clearly calls for all men and women everywhere to live as if they are one blood.

The Phenomenon of Majority

History reveals that racism is a deep and abiding curse supported by a long-standing condition that has bred a natural phenomenon more potent and subtle than racism itself. I call it the "phenomenon of majority." Over time, racial privilege and advantage become part of the pedigree of the majority race. Any solution, therefore, must go at least as deep as the historical and root causes of the problem.

In the case of the United States of America, racism was written into the highest laws of the land. The founding fathers were white males who intentionally defined terms and wrote laws that conserved rights, powers, and privileges to the exclusion of nonwhite races. The laws were written into what could be called the DNA of the new nation.

The Constitution essentially codified the definitions for slavery, citizenship, and human rights. Its construction was intentional and achieved the intended effect: to enfranchise the majority race and disenfranchise the minority races. More specifically, the rules were written to protect and perpetuate the enfranchisement of wealthy whites, a historical continuation of social stratification inherited from the Middle Age feudal systems of kings, queens, lords, barons, peons, and serfs.

For example, until as recently as 1952, the various naturalization acts written by Congress still allowed only white persons to be naturalized as citizens, except for two years in the 1870s (which the Supreme Court later declared to be a mistake). The Naturalization Act of 1795 set the initial parameters on naturalization: free white persons who had been residents for five years or more. The enabling legislation, which expanded the Fourteenth Amendment by allowing naturalization of "aliens of African nativity and persons of African descent," was the Page Act of 1870 (encyclopedia.jrank. org/articles/pages/ 6061/Citizenship-and-Race.html).

In the early days of our nation, without the protection of an external government, blacks and Native Americans were powerless to defend themselves against the sophisticated militia of invading whites endorsed and supported by the power of the English crown. Blacks soon became the slaves of choice, as they were more visible and vulnerable to permanent servitude.

William J. Wilson writes the following in his book *Power, Racism, and Privilege*:

> Unlike Blacks, Indians, being indigenous to the American colonies, knew a great deal about the territory in which they might seek refuge, and they were organized tribally and thus better able to resist colonial encroachment. In short, they were far less vulnerable to institutionalized White repression than were the Blacks, who were forced to live in a foreign land, lacked organization, and were scattered about the countryside. However, to suggest that Blacks were ultimately chosen over Indians to be enslaved because the slave transfer situation made them much more powerless than the American Indians, is not to ignore the fact that the American Indians' cultural experience rendered them less suitable as slaves. Eric Foner has discussed this issue: "It is one of the tragic ironies of Afro-American history that Africans were imported to the New World because their level of culture and economic skill made them better slave

laborers than the Indians. In fact, African slaves introduced techniques of tropical farming and mining which were adopted by the Europeans." (p. 75)

On the other hand, blacks were legally excluded from participating in the wealth their slave labor created. The disenfranchisement of blacks under the cover of state and federal laws ensured a labor-intensive subculture that lasted legally for two centuries and, in my opinion, has lasted illegally to this very day.

This disenfranchisement is illustrated in the 1819 passage of the Missouri Literacy Law, which forbade the assembling or the teaching of black slaves to read or write. Georgia followed suit in 1829. Alabama and Virginia also passed literacy laws that fined and flogged whites for teaching blacks to read or write.

In most states in both the North and the South, laws existed that severely prohibited or restricted blacks from freedom of movement, marriage, business ownership, education, voting, or even living in the state as free men (Harriet C. Frazier, *Runaway and Freed Missouri Slaves and Those Who Helped Them; 1763–1865; Jefferson, NC; McFarland; 2004; p. 8.*) How, in the name of fairness, is this not a great argument for some form of affirmative action?

The Supreme Court's infamous Dred Scott decision of 1857 constitutionally dehumanized and disenfranchised an entire race. The occurrence and severity of such laws are well documented and too numerous to mention for our purposes here. But the point is, racism in America has been institutionalized and legalized for centuries and is directly responsible for ensuring that power would remain in the control of the majority race. This institutionalized and legalized majority has, over time, directly influenced black self-concept, self-esteem, social status, criminal justice and worldview.

The leaders of these institutions have often produced self-serving studies, tests, and scientific evaluations to "prove" the intellectual or genetic superiority of whites over blacks. However, just as many studies, tests, and books have been written to prove such literature spurious at best.

One such example of this kind of self-serving study is *The Bell Curve,* written in 1994 by Richard J. Hernstein and Charles Murray. We know now that the so-called science used was heavily weighted with results obtained from narrow, culturally based data gathered, written, and interpreted by whites for whites, with predictable findings resulting. In one such attempt to correct the record, Grace Carlson writes:

> Why then have modern historians been silent about the high cultural attainments of the black peoples of ancient Ethiopia, glowing accounts of which have been preserved in the writings of such Greek and Roman historians as Homer (ninth century B.C.), Herodotus (fifth century B.C.), Pliny (first century A.D.), and Ptolemy (second century A.D.)? Why have the roles of Negro

blood and ancient Negro culture been denied their proper place in the historical explanations of the development of Egyptian civilization? Because, as Professor DuBois correctly points out, the needs of the white slave traders of the 16th, 17th and 18th century Europe and the United States made it necessary to distort and hide all favorable facts and interpretations of the history of the black peoples. (Grace Carlson from Fourth International, *The Myth of Racial Superiority*, vol. 5, no.1, January 1944, pp. 17–21)

The world-renowned scholar and writer W. E. B. DuBois wrote:

The whole attitude of the world was changed to fit this new economic reorganization. Black Africa, which had been a revered example to ancient Greece and the recognized contender with imperial Rome, became a thing beneath the contempt of modern Europe and America. All history, all science was changed to fit this new condition. Africa had no history. Wherever there was history in Africa or civilization, it was of white origin; and the fact that it was civilization proved that it was white. If black Pharaohs sat on the throne of Egypt, they were really not black men but dark white men. Ethiopia, land of the blacks, was described as a land of the whites.... If at any time, anywhere there was evidence in Africa of the human soul and the same striving of spirit, and the same build of body found elsewhere in the world, it was all due to something non-African and not to the inherent genius of the Negro race. (Black Folk, Then and Now; New York; Henry Holt and Company; 1939; p. 221)

Almost two centuries later, the mental, emotional, and psychological scars inflicted by this action remain unpurged by the available unpublished offsetting science and laws of equal consequence, national repentance, or reparations for the millions of lives lost in that African holocaust called the Middle Passage.

The intentional tearing apart of families in slavery and selling them off like car parts in a junkyard, as well as the deliberate infliction of terror and humiliation designed to break the wills and brainwash the minds of slaves in order to ensure their submission and destroy their self-esteem, left a lingering and devastating mark. Their cursed generations of survivors have been labeled "minorities" because they are lesser in number and, according to the Constitution of the ruling majority (the Dred Scott decision), lesser as human beings.

The phenomenon of majority is the passive perpetuation of privilege and power to a racially specific group who, having numerical superiority, exercise and pass it on generationally. Those born to such a majority race inherit innate privilege, inalienable rights of passage, untold wealth, and unspoken benefits by virtue of their birth. They are acculturated to share such power and privilege with their own kind, first and foremost. Now, that is a hard habit to break.

What enabled this phenomenon to work so well in the first place was that it was the legal, cultural, and politically correct expectation for both the majority and the minority. During the days of slavery, the word of a slave held no value or power when spoken against the word of a white person. The word of a white child carried more weight than the word of a black adult. Blacks had a "place" and were required to stay in it. Blacks as well as whites accepted this status quo and would often chide one another to "stay in your place."

Until 1964, the United States, the land of the free and home of the brave, consistently exercised a double standard based on race in regards to voting rights. Blacks had to pay poll taxes, take tests, and perform various other tasks not required of whites. This double standard was extended to other areas and created two opposing mind-sets among both the majority and minority that, I believe, exist to this day.

For instance, whites as a whole view the criminal justice system as fair and impartial, because this is the truth of their experience as members of the majority living with the advantage of the phenomenon of majority. Blacks, on the other hand, as members of the minority, strongly feel that crime is often judged and adjudicated based on color. We even give our children, especially our sons, special instructions about how to drive through certain communities and what to do if stopped by the police. In the black community, it is called being stopped on a "DWB": driving while black.

Another example takes place in our courtrooms. An all-white jury's conviction of a black person is seldom questioned in the white community; however, an all-black jury's conviction of a white person is unlikely to go unchallenged. This phenomenon is not racist in the mind of the majority members, even though it advantages one race over another; but to the minority members, it is blatant racism.

Both blacks and whites would benefit from understanding on a deeper level this phenomenon of majority. Many good and decent whites don't have a clue as to why blacks are angry. Being majority members, they have no reason to question the system that gave them their jobs or accepted their college entrance applications. Their assurance, confidence, and faith in the system often stem from this take-it-for-granted phenomenon of living as a majority member.

But from the black perspective, whites operate by a set of rules that have been written and enforced by—what else— white majority rule. The majority's expectations, hopes, and dreams are shaped by age-old definitions, morals, and values that have been codified and made sacred by time and tradition.

It isn't that majority-race members are not good, nice, decent people; it is simply that they are often good, nice, and decent to their own, first and foremost. It is so consistent that it seems instinctive. I confess,

I may be parsing words here. The phenomenon of majority may indeed be racism by another name. I am suggesting, however, that sometimes it is submerged in a subconscious response to one's traditions, training, and culture and is not a racially premeditated act.

If this is true—and I believe it is—it puts a significantly different spin on how we view those who are innocently caught up in racial majorities and cultures that have systematically subjugated and dominated minorities, and it changes the volatile dynamics of the discussion. Sometimes those in the dominant culture unwittingly and unintentionally say and do things that are completely out of order and hurtful, or interpreted as put-downs by the minority culture. More often than not, I believe, this cultural or racial insensitivity is caused by ignorance, habit, and presumption, but not necessarily racism.

Maybe we need to stop defining each other by the worst possible stereotypes and leave room for error and correction. While I will discuss this phenomenon a little further in chapter 7, I will tell you here and now that I am all for changing language, presumptions, and stereotypical predispositions in order to sustain the dialogue and ultimately reframe perspectives. I am convinced that some things are not racist; they are simply the result of being in the majority for centuries.

Discussion Guide

1. What institution is designed and designated to protect minority rights from the tyranny of the majority?

2. Is the church a democratic institution? Should it be? What is the difference between a democracy and a theocracy?

3. How does the phenomenon of majority relate to social change? From your perspective, describe some benefits of being a majority-race person.

4. When, if ever, is affirmative action appropriate? Discuss the best way to restore what slavery deprived the enslaved of.

Chapter 5

THE PHENOMENON OF MAJORITY AND THE BREEDING OF PERPETUAL PRIVILEGE AND EXCLUSION

Because of the historically entrenched traditions sanctified by the laws of "God-fearing" men, the phenomenon of racism and majority has had far-reaching implications, both in time and grade. In other words, racism gradually became a mutually accepted tradition and belief that one's skin color makes a difference. However, racism's manifestations differed greatly among different majorities. For example, racism in the South was generally regarded as more violent and aggressive than racism in the North. Thus we may need to view what we commonly refer to as racist or racism from a more pragmatic perspective.

For generations, certain races were raised to believe they were born into a world of automatic privilege and entitlement. At early ages, they were regaled with stories of the exploits, triumphs, and dominion of their ancestry. This phenomenon-of-majority syndrome produced an official written record of history that reflected a majority truth; that is, truth based solely on biased or even untrue claims.

For example, if one were to ask, "Who discovered America?" the average person, black or white, would answer, "Columbus." All of us were taught as fact that Columbus discovered America, yet there is voluminous literature to the contrary; *They Came Before Columbus-The African Presence in Ancient America by Ivan Van Sertima; 1421 by Gavin Menzies and Before Columbus by Sharon Fabian to name a few.* History is always written by the majority culture and almost always reflects the truth as told by that culture.

Throughout history, many who were members of the dominant culture inherited legacies of treasure, both ill gotten and legitimate, real and imagined. They almost always established dominant-culture rules that perpetuated their privilege and guaranteed their dominance. This appears to be true whether the dominant culture was Native American, African, or the infamous European feudal system of medieval times, which some believe was the breeding ground for slavery, classism, and ultimately racism as we know it today.

The ancient clans of European dynasties were built upon the backs of peasants, or serfs, who were tied to the land and owned by barons and lords. No matter the origin, these lucky lords were entrenched, entitled, and generational, and they enjoyed the dominance of class, culture, and race. The offspring of the privileged, whether feudal lord, slave master, or family member of the ruling tribe, rarely questioned their good fortune; and, really, why should they? Through no fault of their own, they were born into a system in which they and those who looked liked them automatically had power and privilege. Contrarily, others were born into a system in which those who looked like them were regarded as nothing more than chattel with very few individual human rights.

The truth is, the saying that power concedes nothing is really a fact of life — not racism. The offspring of the slave master knew no other way. They were bred to believe that they were the leaders because they were superior. Consequently, as suggested in the previous chapter, much of what is today called racism may actually be the phenomenon of majority: the belief that a group is superior because it is the majority.

The expectations and experiences resulting from centuries of being citizens of the majority instruct that majority to hold a self-serving worldview that includes some and excludes others. Racial superiority is as much a generational curse as racial inferiority. In fact, in the grand scheme of things, it is not so much the race that matters as it is who is lucky enough to be born into the majority race or unlucky enough to be born into the minority race.

As a black man, if I believe that a white person has treated me unfairly because of his conditioning as a member of a racial majority and not because of personal hatred, I gain an entirely different perspective that makes it easier to hope for change. I begin to recognize that being born into privilege and power carries with it a handicap toward understanding others, especially minority cultures. It explains to me how whites can say and do racist things ignorantly, not understanding the origins of their own perceptions and assumptions.

However, if I include this victim of the phenomenon of majority in the same class as the white supremacist, I remove all margin for human error and eliminate the incentive to negotiate, since the white supremacist believes "the only good nigga is a dead nigga." What is the difference between the two? One hates me because I am black; the other loves me because he perceives me as inferior. While their behaviors may be similar, their motivations are quite different.

There is hope that the white phenomenon-of-majority person can and will be rehabilitated, because we can reason together, get to know each other's histories and journeys, and thus change our minds. My chance for being reconciled with the white supremacist, however, is hindered by something neither of us can change: color. He hates me because I am black. He is dangerous, and sooner or later, unless I first convert him, I will be forced to kill him in self-defense, since he is dedicated to killing me.

But could this phenomenon of majority explain why it seems at times that whites are blind to cause and effect and often ask, quite puzzled, "What do they want?" or in the case of trying to understand what prompted the attacks of 9/11, "Why do they hate us so?" Sadly, this type of question is often asked with no intention of waiting for the answer from "them," because whatever "they" say has already been marginalized and minimized as minority opinion subject to the definitions and interpretations of the dominant culture.

This racial and cultural conditioning has created a seemingly impenetrable wall of insensitivity. Among my many friends of the dominant culture who constantly exercise their privilege in my presence, I notice a total blackout of their understanding of me and my perception or reaction to a given moment or incident. I often find myself explaining to them what just happened. When I do, I find that they were totally oblivious, clueless, and innocent of any premeditation or ill will.

Did You See That?

The phone rang in my office one sunny afternoon. My secretary informed me that a gentleman from a major corporation wanted to speak with me regarding charges of racism made against the corporation by a group of black pastors in metropolitan Los Angeles. I consented, and the next day two white men in their early forties met me at my office. From there we proceeded to a nice Pasadena restaurant.

We quickly got to the point of our meeting, and the two men began to pour their hearts out, explaining that they did not understand where the charge of racism had come from. During this time, the waiter came by with menus for each of us. He patiently and professionally described the daily special to Jim and Martin (not their real names) before very courteously turning to me and doing the same — only this time taking great care to also inform me of the cost of each item.

As the waiter left the table, I said to my guests, "Did you see that?"

Martin looked at Jim and then looked around the restaurant before responding, "What? What happened? What did I miss?" Jim was equally as clueless and wanted to know what I was talking about.

"Did you notice that the waiter informed only me of the cost of each item?" I asked.

"You are absolutely right!" Jim exclaimed, registering both alarm and embarrassment. "I did notice he was a little condescending, but I didn't think too much of it," he admitted.

I scooted my chair closer to the table, rubbed my hands together, and said, "Okay, let's talk." I began to explain: "The most important thing to remember is that you didn't *hear* the waiter make the distinction. The second most important thing for you to know is that black people are the most paranoid people in the world. We see race, if not racism, in everything. The baggage that any of us bring to any relationship affects the relationship. In this case, my baggage is the paranoia, and your baggage is presumption. One more thing, I'll bet you the check, which Pasadena Church of God is paying, that the waiter gives you — not me — the check."

Jim eagerly replied, "You're on!" Now actually that was a bad bet, since the mathematical odds were in my favor; however, it did make for good conversation. When the waiter gave the bill to Jim without even asking any questions, I could hardly continue my ninety-minute racial-sensitivity session because I was laughing so hard.

Jim and Martin laughed too, but their faces glowed bright red. They were embarrassed because they thought they were part and parcel of a racist event. They thought I was hurt. Instead, it provided a perfect teaching moment—*if they were open to learn and not just intent on winning.* I explained that what we had just witnessed was racially motivated, but not racist. I asserted my belief that the waiter was acting from his conditioning and acculturation, as was the financial institution that had sent them to me.

It was a powerful moment.

As we continued our conversation, I shared with them the sad truth of redlining, the discrimination in housing and insurance that plagues so many in the black community. We also talked about the cultural conflicts and language barriers that distort the understanding between the weak and the powerful, the privileged and the underprivileged. At the end of a good meal and great conversation, Jim and Martin shook my hand, thanked me for lunch and an epiphanous experience, and promised to stay in touch.

The next time I heard from them was in a letter denying our proposal for H.O.M.E (Home Owning Made Easy), a plan completely backed by cash on deposit at their institution. Although our members could get loans to buy Cadillacs, they could not get cash-secured down payments for houses, thus the need for the proposal. After receiving the denial letter, I remember leaning back in my chair, thinking, *Power and privilege concede nothing. It's time for the Molotov cocktail!*

Jim and Martin were highly placed officers in a large financial institution. They appeared to be ready for social and policy change that would empower the minority communities, but their bond to traditional institutional thinking was strong, having developed over many years. Simply put (albeit, over simply), it was their breeding, both economic and racial, that prompted their response.

Jim and Martin did what their fathers had taught them: smile, be friendly, let others talk, and be sensitive—but never balance the equation at your own expense. At all costs, maintain your privilege and power. Of course, you will not find this racial mor`e recorded in any book in a public library. It is, nonetheless, a very real perception emanating from very real experiences over several centuries of breeding on both sides.

There is, therefore, a genuine innocence that belongs to the offspring of the privileged who were born into majority status. We all learned in high school physics that for every action there is an equal and opposite reaction. I might add that in addition to the reactions being equal and opposite, they are also either positive or negative. In the case of the dominant culture, the negative reaction comes from being falsely accused of racism. In the case of the victim, the negative reaction is to turn to violent overthrow of whatever or whoever is perceived to be the perpetrator of the racism.

The positive reaction by those born to majority privilege is to engage in dialogue and discussion without preconditions. They must consciously adopt a posture of learning and understanding both the phenomenon of majority and the resulting pathology of the minority. This necessitates recognizing the "phenomenon of riot," the deep and always-near-the-surface anger and the desperate, soulful need for reparations, which could be as simple and inexpensive as the word *sorry*.

There remain many unanswered questions, but I am sure of one thing. In the twenty-first century, old racist perceptions and realities—no matter the origin or philosophical basis—must be allowed to die. We must starve them of their food—bigotry, prejudice, and ignorance—and make way for a grand and glorious racial reconciliation.

The sovereign, just, and holy God who created each one of us did not leave us without a root-reaching remedy for the disease of a stalking racism that He knew would mock us until His return. Nor did He leave us to the merciful benevolence of racial, gender, political, military, or economic majorities. In the apostle Paul's second letter to the Corinthians, he writes:

> Our firm decision is to work from this focused center: One man died for everyone. That puts everyone in the same boat. He included everyone

in his death so that everyone could also be included in his life, a resurrection life, a far better life than people ever lived on their own. Because of this decision we don't evaluate people by what they have or how they look. We looked at the Messiah that way once and got it all wrong, as you know. We certainly don't look at him that way anymore. Now we look inside, and what we see is that anyone united with the Messiah gets a fresh start, is created new. The old life is gone; a new life burgeons! Look at it! All this comes from God who settled the relationship between us and Him and then called us to settle our relationships with each other.

—2 Corinthians 5:14–18 MSG

And therein lies the answer to racism in America as we know it today. We must apply a brand-new standard of measurement, a new point of view that reaches down to the root causes and favors no status-quo remedies. Peace and justice must marry, and reconciliation must be preceded by change of view and change of heart. One thing is for sure: our hope must not be in our politics, even as we seek political change. We have been there and done that. Self-preservation will always rule our politics. The revival of which I speak must be one of the soul.

Behind the Curtain

History shows that majorities almost always vote in their own best interests. The secrets of the heart are often revealed behind the curtain in the ballot box. In 1983, for example, leading up to the night the late Harold Washington was narrowly elected the first black mayor of Chicago, the polls showed him with a comfortable lead. But when it came time to go behind the curtain, one of the most astounding election nights in American political history unfolded. Democratic whites of the most Democratic city in the country, Chicago, Illinois, voted Republican.

In all fairness, it must be pointed out that Harold Washington won because there were enough whites who got it. Nevertheless, that night confirmed the suspicion of many that, given the proper cover, a conditioned majority would vote their race, which in effect was a vote to preserve power, privilege, and advantage. By definition, such action is racism.

In 1988, who can forget George H. W. Bush's Willie Horton ads, which — at least to blacks — played to racial fears and portrayed Massachusetts governor Michael Dukakis as soft on crime? Many believe it cost Dukakis the election.

In 2006, in an effort to prevent congressman Harold Ford, Jr. from becoming the first black senator from Tennessee, his white conservative Republican opponent played, what seemed to many, a vicious race card. In this provocative television ad, a powerful reminder was sent to white males in particular and whites in general that in order to preserve racial purity, power, and privilege, they should vote their race and not their conscience. A few did, and the strategy proved successful, with Ford losing by a few votes. So consistent is this dirty little habit that the major polls factor in race, especially when the candidates are of a different race. These polls are amazingly accurate because racism is amazingly predictable.

Human Remedies

For blacks, affirmative action is probably the litmus test for identifying white racism. In their viewpoint, to deny the need for affirmative action is like denying the Jewish Holocaust ever happened. To be against affirmative action *without offering a comparable reparation plan* is to deny that serious and egregious wrong was done during slavery and under legal cover for two centuries thereafter and disregards the fact that whites gained tremendous power, privilege, and advantage as a result. To deny significant if not equal redress is by definition racist, where *racism* is defined as "a calculated, deliberate and well-executed plan for the exploitation and subjugation of one people by another for the purpose of securing power and advantage" (Dr. Claud Anderson, Ed.D., *PowerNomics*).

To be unwilling to give back goods acquired illegally, whether property; equal rights under the law; or the rape of dignity, destiny, body, and soul, is racist, immoral, unconscionable, and unchristian. The operative word here is *unwilling,* as I am advocating in this book unconditional reconciliation.

I will agree that an affirmative action that victimizes any people based on race or gender is equally immoral and unjust and will only perpetuate the problem. However, I do not agree that the solution is to end it without remedy. I say, "Amend it—don't end it!" I, for one, could accept a public apology, a national holiday that celebrates diversity, and free college education for all blacks, Native Americans, and women who qualify to go to any college or university they choose for the next two hundred years (four hundred for Native Americans). This, to me, would be victimless affirmative action and an attempt to right the wrongs committed in generations past.

The point? Don't put out the fire but leave the burn victim untreated. Don't just drag the drowning man to shore; do artificial respiration to get the water out of his lungs. Breathe for him until he can breathe on his own.

Historically, secular governments, whether by majority rule or military might, have been unable to bring peace and community in multicultural societies. Racism will never be voted out, because it is essentially a moral problem. And it is almost universally agreed that morality cannot be legislated.

Racism cannot exist unless someone or some group benefits from it and has the power to make the rules that maintain the benefit. How to overcome a historical majority that bends the rules to favor itself is always the problem for the historical minority. For the answer, we must not look to the pyrotechnicians of the 1960s, whose battle cry of "burn, baby, burn" got them absolutely nowhere. Nor can we look to political formations such as the Moral Majority or the Southern Christian Leadership Conference (SCLC). Though these were well-meaning Christian organizations, they polarized the country and the Christian community — all in the name of Jesus.

Religious Remedies

It is my personal observation that well-intentioned parachurch groups have a diminishing shelf life of about four years before they lose their luster and decline in effectiveness. However, if the church (preachers and their congregations) gets involved, it tends to have more dramatic results that last longer.

For example, the civil rights movement of the sixties was primarily church driven. It adopted Christian principles of nonviolence; and its members met in churches, where they worshiped, prayed, and then went out into the streets. This movement, made up of people of all races and denominations, precipitated a revolution that changed this country forever and impacted the entire world.

Although the leaders of the movement were religious people, when they attempted to create a formal organization, their interest and effectiveness soon peaked and faded. This is due to the fact that the transition from spiritual to secular defuses the core values and moral authority of the group. The kingdom of God, or the church, is a live spiritual force whose values do not always translate or transfer well into secular organization. The moral: Let the church be the church.

Political Remedies

Historically, racism derives its strength and authority from democracy and is sanctified by religion. By democracy, I mean a one man–one vote structure coupled with a majority-rule system for policy and lawmaking. This rule by the majority can never eradicate racism in its present form.

In the fledgling days of its innocence, the young America etched into its Constitution the Three-Fifths Compromise. The effect of this was to count, for congressional apportionment purposes, black slaves as three-fifths human. Though such action might seem inconceivable to most of us today, the fact remains that when the majority makes the rules, it will always rule in favor of its own self-interest at the expense of whoever is called the minority. (By the way, I resist owning the term *minority* when referring to myself, as it becomes a self-marginalizing reference with the power to influence and obscure my self-respect, my worldview, and the worldview of those with whom I speak).

In this type of setup, what is considered normal is determined by the majority, and what is considered abnormal (against the norm) is also a determination made by the majority. Under majority rule, the giving and taking of power, privilege, advantage, and opportunity is exercised in either tyranny or in benevolence. When exercised in tyranny, a primary outcome is racism and racial bigotry. When exercised in benevolence, there is humane benefit and a sharing of civility that fosters goodwill and maximizes the gifts and potential of all people. But all too often tyranny seizes the upper hand and forces its dictates upon the powerless.

It's a lot like the humorous story I once heard of a young boy named Johnny. Little Johnny was about to get a spanking. His mother, ever the teacher and determined to make Johnny confess and understand his need for the spanking, asked her son, "Do you know why I am going to spank you?"

Johnny replied quickly, "Yes, I know why I'm getting a spanking."

"Then tell Mommy why."

Without missing a beat, Johnny replied, "Because you're bigger than me."

What we know today is that some people have position, title, or power, not because they are the best qualified, but because they are in the majority—they are the "biggest." It is the *tyranny* of the majority, whether race based, class based, or economics based, that seeds the conditions for violent revolutions, social turmoil, and social crime. No nation with an oppressed underclass can peacefully exist for long.

Indeed, this is the explicit purpose of the Supreme Court: to bring balance to the executive and legislative branches of government, both of which are elected by popular majority. The United States Supreme Court is the voice of the disenfranchised minorities and exists to protect the human rights of those who would otherwise fall victim to a tyrannical majority. When a tyrannical majority rules without check or balance, it soon sows the seed of its own destabilization and ignites a ticking time bomb for violent revolution.

Discussion Guide

1. Give examples when the majority was wrong.

2. What is God's pattern as it relates to the use of majority numbers?

3. Should the U.S. Supreme Court change laws made by a majority? Give examples of Supreme Court decisions that overturned "majority rule." Do such actions qualify as "legislating from the bench" or correcting unconstitutional legislation? Discuss.

4. Should the church flow in majority-rule tradition in obedience to the law of the land, or should it be an instrument of civil disobedience? What should be the church's role in overturning unfair laws?

Chapter 6

A BIBLICAL CASE HISTORY
Majority Rule Versus Minority Favor

The phenomenon of majority is a historical phenomenon that is easily identified in Bible history. The biblical record could be instructional to all minorities because it shows how God never used majorities to accomplish His purpose. It's almost as if God is saying, "This is My way, and these are My rules." In Deuteronomy 7:7, Moses clearly stated to God's people, "The Lord did not set his love upon you, nor choose you, because ye were more in number than any people; for ye were the fewest of all people" (KJV).

In fact, they were not even the most righteous. Deuteronomy 9:6–7 makes this point quite strongly: "Know this and don't ever forget it: It's not because of any good that you've done that God is giving you this good land to own. Anything but! You're stubborn as mules. Keep this in mind and don't ever forget how angry you made God, your God, in the wilderness. You've kicked and screamed against God from the day you left Egypt until you got to this place, rebels all the way" (MSG).

If the Israelites were few in number, stiff-necked, and rebellious, why would God choose them? The answer: covenant! "But because the Lord loved you, and because he would keep the oath which he had sworn unto your fathers . . ." (Deut.7:8 KJV). This concept of covenant boggles the mind and defies both political and religious reason. But if we miss this point, we are destined to chase our tails trying to qualify for God's grace instead of glorifying Him for His free gift.

Because of God's holiness, He held Israel to a standard of righteousness, and His justice chastised them when they fell short. But no matter how far they strayed, His honor of covenant held on to them. What an awesome God! "Know this: God, your God, is God indeed, a God you can depend upon. He keeps his covenant of loyal love with those who love him and observe his commandments for a thousand generations" (Deut. 7:9 MSG).

Favor "Ain't" Fair: The Journey

The Jews, God's imperfect minority remnant, is a case history of a minority's not- what-you-know-but-who-you-know relationship overcoming majority rule. One cannot help but conclude that odds and conditions do not matter once God speaks. The Jews never seemed to get it right with any reliable consistency, and they were always outnumbered and outgunned; yet always they were the odds-on favorite to win. This smacks of a setup! Somebody is working behind the scenes; somebody knows Somebody. This "ain't" fair!

Throughout history, God has suffered majorities to rule and has used majority rule as a teaching tool for an elect remnant that was always in the minority. The third chapter of the book of Joshua is the culmination of the story of four hundred years of Jewish slavery. The generation that was poised to crossed over the Jordan into the Promised Land was more than a millennium removed from the original events that had led to this momentous occasion. Until now, they had held on to the stories of their forefathers and dreamed of this day of freedom, prosperity, and having a place of their own (sound familiar?).

To the Israelites, this crossing the Jordan into the Promised Land was the most significant event in their history in over a thousand years. It was the fulfillment of God's promise to Abraham, Isaac, and Jacob, the patriarchs of this "called out" and peculiar minority people. A famine had originally brought them into a foreign land where they became slaves for over four hundred years. Slavery, with its incumbent behavior and attitudes, was all they knew. As far back as any one of them could remember, they had been slaves. Slavery, slave behavior, slave expectations, slave planning, and even slave dreaming were all they had ever known. They even prayed and worshiped like slaves. By the fifth generation and after two hundred years of slavery, the idea of freedom was reduced to dreaming the impossible dream. By the tenth generation and after four hundred years of slavery, any notion of God being for them had perished in the reality of their endless bondage.

By this point, no one alive knew what it was like to be free. Ten generations had been born and bred in slavery. Their expectations of themselves, their leaders, and their children were contaminated and shaped by their slave mentality. Their frame of reference, their standard of living, their style of government (theocracy), and their religion were affected by their past and reinforced by their present condition. Consequently, when Moses appeared on the scene, not all of the Jews were convinced that independence was the way to go. To many of them, Moses was a flawed fugitive troublemaker. It took ten plagues and a death angel to convince everyone it was in their best interest to follow Moses out of Dodge.

So entrenched were their emotions and fears, they were afraid to be free. This mind-set persisted, even after they followed their leader out of Egypt and stood poised to take possession of what God had promised. When faced with the challenge, they questioned their leaders and prophesied their own doom, believing they were better off under their majority rulers: "We can't attack those people; they are stronger than we are. . . . We seemed like grasshoppers in our own eyes, and we looked the same to them. . . . Wouldn't it be better for us to go back to Egypt?" (Num. 13:31, 33; 14:3). Though Abraham, their greatest of predecessors, would become known as the father of faith millenniums later, they still did not have a clue regarding what faith was or how to use it to their advantage to make life better.

The Egyptians faced no such struggle regarding their abilities or leadership. After four hundred years of enslaving and dominating the Jews, they were convinced of their own superiority and the Jews' inferiority. After all, they had never seen it any other way. They were not intentionally arrogant; they simply oozed with the confidence of four hundred years as masters of all they surveyed. Four hundred years in leadership, four hundred years with the best jobs, four hundred years of being first, four hundred years of going to the head of the line had cultivated and entrenched their views of both themselves and their Jewish slaves.

Here's the Deal

A step back in time may help us to put the struggle of this minority group in better perspective. The Jews were not some physiologically exclusive race of people favored above others because of their ancestry, the shape of their nose, or the hue of their skin. The fact is, God made a deal with Abram: "The Lord had said to Abram, 'Leave your country, your people and your father's household and go to the land I will show you; I will make you into a great nation and I will bless you; I will make your name great, and you will be a blessing. I will bless those who bless you, and whoever curses you I will curse; and all peoples on earth will be blessed through you" (Gen. 12:1–3).

The deal God made with Abram (soon to be Abraham) was an inclusive covenant that would bless all peoples on earth. These covenant people were a holy remnant taken from a common ancestry with whom they shared the same DNA. The only difference between Abraham and some of his descendants was that Abraham was the one who took the deal. He cut a deal with Jehovah, and even though he did not fully understand what God was up to, he took the deal and thus became the father of faith.

Abraham was originally just a good old Gentile, if you please—nobody special; no blue blood, just red. He entered into a sacred covenant with God and together with Sarah started a lineage through which God Himself would be born as flesh and blood in the person of Jesus the Christ, thus fulfilling man's need of an unblemished-by-sin sacrifice—a perfect Savior.

The Jews were a new covenant family, a supernatural creation that began with Abram and Sarah's entering into covenant with God and then having a baby named Isaac by way of a double reproductive miracle. Ultimately, because of this covenant, the Savior of all humankind came into the world and fulfilled God's prophecy from ages past: "And I will put enmity between you and the woman, and between your offspring and hers; he will crush your head, and you will strike his heel" (Gen. 3:15).

Such were the historical circumstances and the background of Moses and the ragtag group emerging from the wilderness after forty years of wandering. After four hundred years of slavery and forty years of wandering on a journey that should have taken only forty days, they finally stood poised and positioned on the brink of seeing the promise fulfilled.

Then tragedy struck: Moses died! There was a sudden change of leadership and paradigms. Gone were the cloud by day and pillar of fire by night. As spectacular as that had been, it was over. Now Joshua, a much younger man, along with the priests and the ark of the covenant, would lead the Jews. Numerically, they were the same minority that had left Egypt, but everything else, it seemed, had changed.

The only thing standing between them and paradise was a river, but it was at flood stage. However, God, their difference maker and their majority of one, miraculously held back the waters of the Jordan, allowing them to cross over and ultimately to prevail. They prevailed in spite of their numbers. They prevailed in spite of their four hundred years of imposed inferiority. They prevailed in spite of the supposed superiority of more sophisticated enemies. They prevailed because they honored Jehovah and embraced His purpose for them. Through their ultimate obedience to the covenant, they walked into the covenant blessings made to their forefathers and fulfilled generations later in them.

Take the Deal

We are all set free by the truth. Freedom at all levels begins with knowing the truth, and the truth begins with God. Whatever state we find ourselves in, we must discover the truth of how we got there before we can get out and stay out. Ignorance is the enemy of the enslaved and the ally of the slave master. One cannot be dominated, subjugated, or enslaved without cooperating with the perpetrator.

In the Middle East today, Israel is the numerical minority, but the power majority. Ironically, both Palestinians and Jews are enslaved by their ignorance. Enslaved to their hatred and their ignorance of the new covenant, the Palestinians fight for an ancient cause that is no longer valid in modern terms. The Jews are enslaved to their self-righteous and equally ancient assumption that they have a divine right to a land and a city that were both prophetic types. Their notions of sharing and forbearing are held hostage to their ignorance of the twenty-first-century truth that war begets war.

Unfortunately, both groups are aided and abetted by Christians who have misinterpreted Scripture and, in the name of their parochial perspective, favor one above the other. The truth, however, is that both groups are wrong. They are both holding the proverbial lion by the tail and live captive in a vicious cycle of fear and war.

They can choose to continue in this path and die in their hatred and the blood puddles of their madness, or they can embrace the Messiah and began to live under the new covenant blessings of love, forgiveness, acceptance, and reconciliation. As long as they cling to their ancient beliefs, however, they will live by the sword and thus die by it. Living under a covenant inferior to the new covenant, they prove to us all that to live by the law is to die by the law.

The entire paradigm for human redemption changed with Jesus' coming to earth and subsequent death on the cross. His death and resurrection irrevocably changed history and historical claims. It fulfilled and finished the old will and covenant and in its place established the new will and covenant. As Abram took the deal offered him at Haran and launched the long journey that included the fulfillment of many promises, so also must we take the New Testament deal of all-out reconciliation in order to experience rest from war and enjoy the dividends of peaceful coexistence.

We experience some of the promises of the new covenant today, not the least of which is announced in Hebrews 11:9–10: "By an act of faith he lived in the country promised him, lived as a stranger camping in tents. Isaac and Jacob did the same, living under the same promise. Abraham did it by keeping his eye on an unseen city with real eternal foundations — the City designed and built by God" (MSG).

This city is the kingdom Daniel saw in King Nebuchadnezzar's dream. He prophesied that what Abraham had seen by faith would happen during the time of the Christ: "In the time of those kings, the God of heaven will set up a kingdom that will never be destroyed, nor will it be left to another people. It will crush all those kingdoms and bring them to an end, but it will itself endure forever" (Dan. 2:44).

Jesus announced this kingdom in Matthew 16:18, explained it in John 3:3–5, and launched it on the day of Pentecost in Acts 2. Because Abraham took the deal in

Genesis 12, you and I walk in it today under a new and better covenant.

The point is, this new covenant is inclusive of all who believe it—period. Under the new covenant, we are all Abraham's seed. The Jew who is born a Jew in the flesh is absolutely no different from the Palestinian or the Gentile who does not believe. Each has equal access. Each is the son or daughter of Abraham. Each is a spiritual heir to the promise and included in the covenant, the last will and testament. Proud histories notwithstanding, each must be born of the Spirit, not the flesh. By faith each becomes the fulfillment of God's eternal strategy: to reconcile men and women to Himself through Christ.

No majority can save any of us. Besides, as believers, we constitute a number no man can number. According to the Scriptures, "a man is a Jew if he is one inwardly; and circumcision is circumcision of the heart, by the Spirit, not by the written code" (Rom. 2:29). This passage is the bridge between the New and the Old Testaments and between promise and fulfillment. It makes me want to say to the Jews and the Palestinians what my mother used to say to break up a noisy argument or fight between us kids: "Okay, that's enough! Stop right now, or no one will eat dinner!"

So to every kind of division, whether black and white, chauvinist and feminist, East Indian and Pakistani, Jew and Arab, Armenian and Turk, Muslim and Christian, Shiite and Sunni, Hispanic and African American, Korean and Japanese, and to all other race-based, nationality-based, color-based, gender-based adversaries, I say, "Get over yourselves! Put your pride in your pocket, and go somewhere and sit down. Stop right now, or no one will eat dinner!"

Jesus' holy, innocent, and royal blood was shed for every wrongful deed, every wrongful death, and every mean and evil thing ever done to any of us. He alone has opened a pathway to mercy, grace, and peace. I exhort you to take the deal. If you take the deal, heaven begins here and now, and the kingdom comes on earth as it is in heaven—right here, right now.

The Bible clearly declares that God's children are His by grace through faith, not by race. Therefore, the rule that governs and determines God's favor is the rule of faith— not majorities, be they political, power, racial, or economic. It is also clear that this plan for humanity predates the dark and demonic divisions we experience today. Abraham was always the father of us *all.* "Consider Abraham: 'He believed God, and it was credited to him as righteousness.' Understand, then, that those who believe are children of Abraham. The Scripture foresaw that God would justify the Gentiles by faith, and announced the gospel in advance to Abraham: 'All nations will be blessed through you' " (Gal. 3:6–8).

I have begun to think there will never be peace in the Middle East until both sides realize the paradigm has shifted. Both sides must recognize the futility of a violent eye-for-an-eye vengeance and instead embrace the Savior, who operates from the new paradigm of the Spirit. Then together with all the citizens of the New

Jerusalem, which is the New Testament kingdom of God, they will find the unity and acceptance that has eluded them for centuries. In this grand and glorious kingdom, "there is neither Jew nor Greek, slave nor free, male nor female, for you are all one in Christ Jesus. If you belong to Christ, then you are heirs according to the promise" (Gal. 3:28–29).

I am almost convinced that even many Christians don't get it. Sometimes those who make the loudest clamor are the greatest perpetrators of religious and racial division. I cease to be amazed at the bigotry and divisiveness of many so-called conservative evangelicals who write off entire nationalities and view entire communities as being doomed or damned and undeserving of even civil rights, while at the same time attempting to win them to a "loving Savior." Give me a break!

I choose to advocate for the Jesus who met the infamous woman at the well, whose religion was different and who had been married five times and was shacking with number six, but saved her anyway. The Jesus I know met a woman caught in the act of adultery, surrounded by accusing religious people ("peeping toms") , and saved her anyway. This Jesus is the same one who defied religious tradition by healing on the Sabbath and who knowingly served communion to the man who would betray Him and the one who would deny Him. The thing is, this same Jesus offers the same deal to us today. Take the deal!

Discussion Guide

1. What are the primary differences between the new and old covenants?

2. What advantage does the new deal have over the old deal?

3. How did four hundred years of slavery affect the Jews?

4. How do you account for the success of the Jews, given their enslavement for four hundred years?

God of our Weary Years • *Dr. M. Tyrone Cushman*

Chapter 7

WHEN THE MAJORITY LISTENS

Presumption

Perhaps one of the most powerful lessons a majority-race person, group, or government can ever learn is what Dr. John Drakeford so aptly describes in his book *The Awesome Power of the Listening Ear*. Listening is a prerequisite to learning, whether in the home or in the classroom. While the poor and the impotent listen by force to the rich and the powerful, listening to the complaint of the weak, the poor, and the defenseless is often treated with benign neglect by those in the majority race. This basic lack of communication is probably at the root of relational disenchantment found in divorce and divisions of all kinds.

The rantings and outrageous remarks made by white celebrities such as Michael Kramer, the comedian who in 2006 blasted a black heckler with racial slurs, are *believed* by most blacks to be real and representative. Equally real are the fears, rage, and flat-out hatred pent up inside so many Native Americans, Hispanics, Arabs, Iraqis, Iranians, Japanese, and any other minority judged and defined by a powerful majority. Because majorities are not in the habit of listening to and valuing the heartfelt cry of the minorities, it is imperative that they ask, "Why do they hate us so?"

The United States of America is the only country in the world that has dropped an atomic bomb on a civilian population. In 1945, in Hiroshima, Japan, 140,000 civilians were killed. Two days later in Nagasaki, Japan, another atomic bomb, nicknamed Fat Man, killed 74,000 civilians – 60,000 of whom were killed instantly. On 9/11, the United States suffered the tragic loss of 3,000 innocent civilians. Looking at sheer numbers, is there any comparison? Which action was the more brutal? Which civilians were the more innocent? Yet we continue to bewilderedly ask, "Why do they hate us so?"

I realize these are not popular statements, and I also realize that some will have a hard time reading this. My purpose is not to get into a discussion of the political expediency or necessity of these actions. I will leave that to the historians. My point is simply that the actions of the majority – right or wrong – always have far-reaching repercussions upon the minority that in turn instigate behavior and reactions misunderstood by the majority.

During the civil rights revolution of the sixties – after the lynchings, after the burnings, after the shootings, after the Birmingham commissioner of public safety Bull Connor's dogs attacked a peaceful demonstration, and after four little black girls were blown up by a bomb planted in their church — massive demonstrations erupted around the country. While blacks could not understand such hate-filled actions, many whites were asking the insulting question I heard with my own ears, "What do they want?"

It is at this precise point that I beg you to keep reading. Attempt to walk with me in the shoes of racial minorities whose hearts have been hardened by the sight of beheaded and castrated loved ones left hanging from a tree, whose only offense was to look a white person in the eye. Yes, I want to share your grief and comfort your loss, but you must understand that for every question you ask, there is an answer. Sometimes, however, the answer is as tragic and cold as the bodies we bury. Why do they hate us? Because they perceive that we hate them. It's that simple. The task before us is to change the hearts and perceptions of those who hate for any reason.

As horrified as I was while watching the Twin Towers fall in real time on that fateful day in September 2001, as soon as it was verified that this was the diabolical work of terrorists, I thought I knew why they did it. Now please understand. In no way am I supportive of the actions of those who resort to terrorism for whatever reason. But when we ask the question, why do they hate us so? with a sincere desire to know the answer, we will find the solution that ends this madness.

Neither our money, nor our laser-guided smart bombs, nor our superior air power, nor the best military soldiers in the world can protect us from a determined enemy with a cause so strong he will commit suicide to exact his revenge. After all, one man's terrorist is another man's freedom fighter.

For centuries the dominant culture has enjoyed the luxury of ignoring powerless minorities. It was only a matter of time before the privilege and power to ignore the impotent would be exercised at the peril of the dominant. It is a phenomenon unique to dominant cultures that causes them not to listen or, even when listening, not to hear. It is the attitude shown by a principal of a private school who bragged to me regarding his meeting with angry black parents: "I just let them talk until they were through. They just needed to vent."

It is the height of arrogance to refuse to negotiate with the impotent and the angry. We ignore at our own peril the cry of the excluded. When pushed to the edge, a 9/11 becomes the only way some who perceive themselves as impotent can be heard. Again, I'm not saying that's right—I'm just saying that's how it is.

It should be noted that only days after 9/11, President Bush, for the first time, called for the institution of a Palestinian state. This new awakening was even more evident in the policy switch by the Bush administration towards the radical Shiite cleric Muqtada Sadr. *The Washington Post Foreign Service* reported on Friday, March 16, 2007: "For Sadr, it is the latest stage in an evolution from populist cleric to guerrilla fighter to political kingmaker and now to power broker. In the early months of the occupation, U.S. officials dismissed Sadr as irrelevant to Iraq's future. Today, they view him as a political catalyst who can help keep Iraq together — or implode it."

What caused the administration to change its attitude? The Muslim cleric's militia raised such a commotion that they were finally heard. To the credit of the administration, they listened, they heard, they negotiated, and peace returned to Sadr City.

We, whether the dominant country or race, cannot continue to claim majority privileges and rights without being perceived as oppressors. We continue the policy of "might makes right" at our own peril. We absolutely must wage peace with our money and our privilege. Technology has made the world too small to peacefully coexist with classism and racism in place.

In 1992, with the acquittal of the Los Angeles police officers in the Rodney King trial, one of the worst riots of the twentieth century erupted. The video of the beating was widely circulated, and the words of a sixties protest chant, "The whole world's watching!" took on new meaning. From that precipitous event and onward, no longer could the majority impose its will, its way of life, its religion, or its politics on proud minorities, no matter how idealistic and well intended — not anymore. Even the political paradigm shifted. Everything changed.

Discussion Guide

1. What do you find difficult about listening to others?

2. Is listening to a perceived enemy a strength or a weakness? Discuss.

3. Why is listening the greatest skill of foreign diplomats?

4. What current events provide evidence that the times have changed and that we fail to listen at our own peril?

PART 2

POLITICS AND THE BLACK EXPERIENCE

Chapter 8

POLITICS IN FLIP-SIDE PERSPECTIVE

The Mind-Set of the Disenfranchised

I remember it as if it were yesterday. The huge Continental Airlines passenger jet lifted off the runway of the Ben Hua airbase in South Vietnam. As the big bird pointed its nose to the sky, the roar of its engines grew louder as it climbed higher and higher. I prayed until we pierced the clouds and lost sight of land. All of us on board held our collective breath until the plane leveled off at thirty-six thousand feet, our cruising altitude. The captain greeted us with words of gratitude and welcome. The stewardesses broke out the champagne. We were going home — we had made it.

We flew to Japan, where we refueled for the long flight to Anchorage, Alaska. There we were allowed off the plane for two hours before boarding for the final leg of our journey to Fort Dix, New Jersey. As soon as we stepped off the plane and onto the Alaskan soil, many of us dropped to our knees and kissed the ground. We cheered, we laughed, and we hugged as we walked triumphantly into the Anchorage terminal.

Here is what I want you to hear and understand: I was glad to be home, but as a young black man, I was not necessarily glad to be an American. I know that will shock some of you, but the truth is, being an American meant more in Vietnam than it did in America. The Vietnamese loved Americans and even seemed to prefer black Americans. And within the military itself, as long as our lives were at stake, race and racial concerns were suspended. The name of the game was "get back to the world alive." But the rules changed for blacks once we got back home. Then it was business as usual.

It was August 1967 when I returned from Vietnam. My hometown of Detroit, Michigan, was still smoldering from the worst rioting in United States history. Just a few years earlier, in 1963, Medgar Evers, a civil rights leader, had been murdered. In that same awful year, four little girls had been murdered in their church bombed by white segregationists. In the case of Medgar Evers, justice did not come until thirty-one years later with the conviction of his assassin. In the case of the four little girls, justice finally came nearly forty years later with the conviction of the last of the four accused (one of the accused died in 1994 without ever having been charged).

Nine months after I returned home from Vietnam, Martin Luther King Jr., world-renowned Nobel Peace

Prize recipient and the greatest of all black American civil rights leaders, was assassinated. That was 1968, and until this day a cloud of doubt and suspicion still hangs over the trial of the convicted assassin.

A long litany of murder and state-supported delay and denial of justice, not to mention the centuries of enslavement of Africans brought to this country in chains, has mocked our nation's glorious claims of liberty and justice for all. In the informed, modern, and educated age of the twentieth century, blacks in the South did not even have the right to vote unhindered by segregationist laws until 1964–65.

The smoldering anger and the bitter memories caused by such harsh realities lived unabated until January 3, 2008, the night of the Democratic Party primary caucus in Iowa. For African Americans, that night was the "end of the beginning" in their age-old struggle. If white Americans, regardless of their political views and opinions, could embrace and understand what that night in particular, and the 2008 election in general, meant to African Americans, it would be the beginning of the end to racism in the United States of America.

The tragedies I listed above are provided to give context to what African Americans felt as they approached the possible election of an African American as president of the greatest nation on earth. Contrast those tragedies with the series of events that led to the election of the first African American president of the

United States and you begin to see wounds healing before your eyes.

Towards a More Perfect Union: Election 2008

The year 2008 will go down in my journal as one of the most exciting years of my life. I dare say it will be recorded as the most important year in all black history. At the risk of being misunderstood, I will tell you that for the first time in my life, I am proud to be an American. Let me explain a little: I am not saying that I wish I had been born somewhere else or that I wish any evil upon the nation of my birth. After all, I did fight in its military and risk my life for its principles. However, as a black American, what did I have as a citizen and as a soldier before 2008? I had public shame, open hurt, deep anger, great sorrow, and patriotic ambivalence.

Proverbs 4:7 says, "With all thy getting, get understanding" (KJV), and this is what should guide our search for racial reconciliation. The need for the dominant race to take the time to listen, learn, and understand the culture, language, and folkways of a minority race is imperative and could not have been demonstrated better than in the case of Barack Obama, the first serious African American candidate for president of the United States.

The entire world was focused on the presidential election of 2008. The world witnessed the testing of a premise put forth by Abraham Lincoln, our sixteenth president, in the Gettysburg Address, possibly the most famous and most quoted speech ever given by a

U.S. president. In that simple yet eloquent document, he said: "Four score and seven years ago, our fathers brought forth on this continent a new nation, conceived in liberty, and dedicated to the proposition that *all men are created equal.* Now we are engaged in a great civil war, testing whether that nation, or any nation, so conceived and so dedicated, can long endure" (emphasis added.)

While the bloodshed of Union and Confederate soldiers officially ended May 5, 1865, the disgrace of another horrid, uncivilized war began—the race war of white versus black and all other nonwhite races. That undeclared war continued until the presidential candidacy of Senator Obama. As a nation, we held our collective breath as we peered into our own souls to see if we had sufficiently bridged the cultural divide to accept a member of a nonwhite race in a new role as president of the United States of America. The question now is, will we judge the new president by the content of his character or the color of his skin?

Interestingly, during the campaign, the story was not about Senator Obama's opponent as much as it was about him. Senator McCain was a white male, and since there had never been anyone other than a white male to run in the general election for president, there was no story there. The news media was primarily focused on Barack Obama, and much of the emphasis was on the fact that he was the first African American candidate ever nominated for the presidency.

As we continue towards the more perfect union Lincoln called for more than 150 years ago, we view with intrigue and frustration how great the divide still is. One incident in the 2008 election demonstrated this quite dramatically. Reverend Jeremiah Wright, the former pastor of Barack Obama, was derided by the press and by many white people who weighed in on the subject for words construed by a white-controlled media to be "unpatriotic," which in the black community is code for "antiblack."

Blacks, on the other hand, were excited and impressed by Reverend Wright's words. After all, he was a great preacher. Hearing him from their context, his words did not strike them as either radical or unpatriotic. We were stunned at the attention and the reaction his sermon received. We felt insulted and misunderstood, as has happened so many times in our history. It was a clear example of cultural and racial misunderstanding.

Until Reverend Wright shamed an otherwise stellar career by displaying an arrogance that was unacceptable by any standard, black America was saying, "He's right," or "I understand where he's coming from, even if I don't agree." However, I want to emphasize — though many whites will struggle to understand — most black Americans, in my opinion, agreed with Jeremiah Wright. But for the sake of political expediency, they could not admit it.

The same principle prevailed in the O. J. Simpson incident, because, in a certain sense, Reverend Wright and O. J. Simpson are the same people. They present an opportunity for black solidarity. They are point men in a cultural jungle. This type of cultural phenomenon occurs beneath the white-awareness radar but helps explain the differences in view.

Because of this minority perception, blacks often find it easier than the majority-race whites to understand cross-cultural frustrations. If you understand Jeremiah Wright, you can understand Yasser Arafat, former Palestinian warrior and president, and, to some extent, even terrorists. It must be remembered that this understanding is independent of approval or agreement with policies and actions, but those who have suffered as minority-race peoples understand others in similar positions in other parts of the world.

When it comes to this type of cross-cultural empathy and understanding, however, most white Americans are handicapped by their majority experience. In other words, if you have never been stopped by the police at night, searched, cursed, and threatened for no reason other than your race, you cannot understand the automatic presumptions and sympathy harbored by minorities who experience those humiliating events on a regular basis. In fact, you probably tend not to believe it even exists. And therein lies the rub.

Our experiences prepare our belief and trust systems. If that is true, you might understand why, as a black man, I was "prepared" to believe that the police could and would set up O. J. Simpson. I was born in distrust and shaped by racial abuse and expectations. I would be the first to agree that I am psychologically damaged by living with so much fear, shame, and negativity. This has been my legacy, unfortunately.

But back to Jeremiah Wright. It was amazing and maddening to hear otherwise intelligent men and women weigh in on the style, meaning, inference, and emphasis of a culture-based sermon that could be understood properly only from a black perspective. Most of the reporters and pundits had never attended a black church in the hood, where a different language is spoken and a different style of worship is practiced. The entertaining, didactic, and prophetic style of preaching that is so prominent and dominant in black churches was foreign territory for most of them.

Whites in general, and an irreligious white media in particular, have no clue of the importance of the black sermon as a tool, a weapon, and an instruction in righteousness, as well as its ability to expose and answer racism. Nor can whites appreciate the black community's picture of patriotism as a white person wrapped in the flag, a justification for privilege and advantage. I know it is a stretch for whites to comprehend why so many blacks do not wave the flag and get teary-eyed or sentimental when "The Star-Spangled Banner" is played. Nevertheless, we served and died valiantly in every war ever fought by this great nation—even when it only enhanced the power and privilege of the majority race. I know that is difficult for many whites to understand, much less accept.

I think I am just trying to say that there is a flip side to majority-held political opinion and perspective that seems to be generally and habitually ignored.

The Peril of Racial Presumption: Bill Clinton

As blacks, we stood by in amazed anger and disappointment as our beloved former first "black" president, William Jefferson Clinton, attempted, in our view, to minimize Barack Obama's candidacy in the South Carolina primary. By implying that a win by either Obama or Jesse Jackson would be because of their race, he minimized them as individuals and all blacks by extension. As to be expected, this incident was viewed very differently by blacks and whites. Even though it involved a person that blacks generally believe to be nonracist, Clinton's comments drove home the point that he and many like him assume their self-declarations of racial neutrality exempt them from the phenomenon of racial conditioning.

From the black perspective, most believed that President Clinton played to what he knew in his soul was his ace card. That card was the race card and the use of culturally coded terms intended to appeal to the racial pride or fear of whites. He did it by pretending it was he who was attacked racially. Because his wife was losing on the issues, he hoped to change the conversation and make the election about race.

Perhaps the inference that was most damaging was President Clinton's minimizing of the value of the black vote. Ignoring the win in Iowa, he suggested that Obama could win only in states where there was a large black constituency. It was as if he called us out. The black community responded with a unity of purpose not seen since the civil rights marches of the sixties. History may well point to Bill Clinton's comment as the turning point in the battle in the primaries.

The main lesson learned from this political misstep is the sin of racial presumption: assuming that one's majority status and one's minority favor can be used at will for one's own benefit. The black community was deeply offended by Clinton's remarks and began to register and vote in record numbers in Florida, Georgia, Mississippi, North Carolina, Maryland, and Virginia. It must be noted, however, this offense did not prick black patriotism as much as it did black pride.

The Everlasting Double Standard

To be fair, I think living in a pluralistic society like the United States presupposes double standards of one kind or another. Nevertheless, if we are to socially understand how racially discriminating assumptions are born, we must carefully note the unrelenting and, more often than not, the unfair scrutiny of minorities who challenge traditional majority-held positions. The candidacy of a black man for the most powerful office in the world exposed not only cultural disparities but also the disparity in the use of words and the interpretation and comprehension of culture-specific language, behavior, religion, and life experience. Each one of these represents powerful cultural differences that may not need to be changed but just understood.

Take, for instance, the comment made by Michelle Obama regarding her pride of country. Not understanding her experience or where she was coming from led to a media feeding frenzy that labeled her as unpatriotic. This was a white reaction to an essentially black comment made from a little-understood black glossary of terms, experiences, and perspectives. Let's look at this more closely.

First of all, black Americans have never ascribed to the "America, right or wrong — love it or leave it" rhetoric used by the flag-waving, self-defining patriots of the sixties. Racism has affected or dominated every waking hour of every black American since they were brought to this country in chains over four hundred years ago. They know that their country has often been wrong, and they have been victims of it.

Second, when Michelle Obama declared, "For the first time in my adult life, I am proud to be an American," she was speaking out of a unique experience. She spoke for nearly every African American in the country over the age of forty, and every African American, regardless of age, understood. However, she made the tactical error of presuming a normal minority-culture expression would be understood by the dominant-culture media and public. Sadly, it was not surprising to see the interpretation of partisan extremism aided by a mercenary media, whose job it is to fan the flames of difference and to assume that their own experiences, definitions, and worldview are the standard by which all others should be judged.

I have lived through six decades of learning how to submerge my instinctive responses to match the expectations of the privileged and the powerful. All my life I have lived in two worlds and have been directly affected by the dominant-culture political opinion and its social folkways and mores. Consequently, being black in America has always impacted me more than simply being American.

As in every culture, African Americans have their own standard of national pride, which for us is based in a unique cultural and historical experience unknown to many in the dominant culture. The definitions for patriotism, national pride, and love of country are as varied and individual as the groups that espouse them. Such definitions are based on unique cultural experiences and do not require agreement or endorsement—just acceptance.

I am sure that most Native Americans and other minority groups share the same reserve of national expression and, like African Americans, are insulted at the arrogance of those who dare define terms for them without sharing the experiences and points of reference that shape their unique perspectives. It's sort of like the dentist who told me that what I was feeling was pressure, not pain. I immediately got out of the chair and walked out of the office before she could inflict more "pressure" on me.

Here is a truth: African Americans do not usually get weepy when they pledge allegiance to the flag. Until November 4, 2008, to us, wearing a lapel pin of the American flag was—and I imagine in a few cases still is—not thought of as patriotic. If you had come into the black community wearing such a pin, you would most likely have been branded a right-wing Republican, not a patriot. So when Michelle Obama was labeled as unpatriotic, it did not resonate with most African Americans, who probably would have echoed her sentiments if given the chance.

Ms. Doris Mitchell, a very dear friend of mine, forwarded to me the following edited e-mail regarding Michelle Obama's statement. I ask you to read it with an open mind in order to understand why, perhaps, she made the statement and why blacks understood it differently from most whites.

> To The Editor:
>
> As a 78-year-old American of African descent, I feel compelled to respond to all this "much ado about nothing" when it comes to the statement that Michelle Obama made about the fact that this is the first time in her adult life that she has been proud to be an American.
>
> The country needs to hear this from the black perspective.
>
> Long before I was born, my grandfather, Joseph Burleson, owned a considerable amount of land in oil-rich Texas. Because during that era blacks could not vote, nor could they contest anything in the courts of the United States, my grandfather's land was *stolen* by his white neighbor. My grandfather, who was literate and better educated

than my grandmother, drove to town. Seeing my grandfather leave, the covetous neighbor asked my grandmother to show him the deed to the property. He snatched it. She could not insist that he give it back, nor could she have reported this *theft* to the sheriff because of the fact that blacks had no rights in the 1800s. The prevailing law at that time was he who held the deed owned the land. Do you think that is something that I am *proud of?* Right now I should be living off the oil and gas royalties [with all the rights and privileges pertaining thereto].

In 1934 when my dad drove us to Texas to meet his family, he stopped to purchase gasoline, and his daughters and wife were not allowed to use the washroom. As a man it was easier for him to relieve himself in the bushes, but not for the females. We were, however, reduced to having to go in the bushes, also. Do you think I am *proud of that?*

In 1938 when my oldest sister went to enroll in Hyde Park High School, she was told by the counselor that she did not want to take college preparatory courses; she wanted to study domestic science. Do you think I'm *proud of that?* Of course, when Beatrice Lillian Hurley-Burleson went to school the next day, that was the last time anyone thought that the Burleson girls wanted to study domestic science. When in 1943 my parents attempted to buy the two-family flat at 5338 South Kenwood, where we had lived since 1933, in Hyde Park, Chicago, Illinois, we were told that we could not buy it because there was a restrictive covenant that said that the property was never to be sold to Negroes. Do you think I am *proud of that?*

In 1950 when I graduated from college, I was unable to get a job because I was considered "over qualified," the code word for they would not hire me because of my race. All of the want ads called for Japanese-Americans, or Nisei (the word given to Japanese-Americans at that time). Do you think that was something that I should have been *proud of?* I understood that America was trying to make up for the interring of innocent and patriotic Americans who were our enemy by association.

My cousin's barbershop was bombed in Mississippi in the '50s because he was encouraging black people to register to vote. His wife, who had earned a master's degree from Northwestern University, lost her position as the principal of the local school because of the voter registration activities. Is that something I should be *proud of?*

We have not seen a phenomenon like Barack Obama in many years and many generations. Like Gandhi, Einstein, Dr. Martin Luther King Jr., and Mother Teresa . . . intellectually and spiritually, these people offer the world so much, but they are often maligned and misunderstood. . . .

. . . So, like Michelle Obama, after living in this country all of my 78 years, loving my country and not understanding why my country has not loved me, I now for the first time in my adult life feel *proud of my country* because I sense a maturing, a recognition of talent and character, and not color, and a field of candidates aspiring to lead this nation coming from very diverse backgrounds of gender, religious beliefs, national origin, ethnicity, age and experiences. This to me is the *hope* that America is coming into her own and will begin to *change* and will embrace the philosophy upon which this country was founded, where all men are created equal and are entitled to life, liberty and the pursuit of happiness. Now I truly believe, *Yes, we can!*

Contact: Helen L. Burleson
Doctor of Public Administration
(708) 747-0919

Now here is the catch: Senator John McCain, the white male candidate, made a statement considered by many to be even more controversial than Michelle Obama's. John McCain on March 13, 2008, while being interviewed by Fox News, said, "I didn't really love America until I was deprived of her company." None of the media, however, picked this up or repeated it over and over as they did Michelle Obama's statement. Why? What was the difference between Michelle Obama's comment and John McCain's? Essentially, there was only one — race.

It cannot be overemphasized that much of Ms. Burleson's experience is shared by the overwhelming majority of all Americans of African descent. The most important thing for whites to understand is that this (the Burleson experience) was a way of life perpetrated upon minorities in general and blacks in particular for many, many years. We were reminded in every way every day that we were not full American citizens. Is it any wonder that our view of the land of our birth differed so sharply from those who had known nothing but the warm embrace and acceptance of the motherland?

Conditioned Black Pride and Patriotism

Throughout our history, when a black man or woman achieved high honor in sports or theater, we celebrated as blacks — not as Americans. When Joe Louis beat Max Schmeling, and when Jesse Owens outran the Germans in front of Adolph Hitler, blacks in America rejoiced more because he was black than because he was American. After all, at one time black athletes had been forbidden to compete against white athletes in the

United States; and even when both Jesse Owens and Joe Louis returned to the States, they did not return as full Americans with equal privileges and rights.

Although both champions, Joe Louis and Jesse Owens, represented their country and represented it well, sadly, their country did not represent them. They returned home to the same old racial insults and Jim Crow laws and limitations. Once they reached the United States, even to the cheers of flag-waving whites, they were still "colored." Without universal voting rights in southern states, they were considered only good enough to entertain, but certainly not intelligent enough to vote or lead. Consequently, intense racial pride was a seamless part of black culture in America as we literally fought and competed on a daily basis for inclusion, recognition, fair treatment, and equal access to power and opportunity.

I am a Vietnam veteran. When I first returned home from the war, I was angry at this unjust war that wasted the lives of over fifty-seven thousand brave young American men and women. A disproportionate number of them were African Americans who could not escape the military draft, like presidents Clinton and Bush and Vice President Cheney had done. For a long time, I refused to stand when the national anthem was played or sung. I have long since repented of my extreme reaction, and I now stand in honor of those who gave their lives; but it is an indication of the anger and hurt that often seethes below the surface in the hearts of many minorities.

During the civil rights struggle of the sixties, I vowed I would not recite the Pledge of Allegiance until some things changed to make my country worthy of such a solemn pledge. The pledge, written by Francis Bellamy in 1892, was designed as an oath of loyalty to the country to be stated in only fifteen seconds. He had initially considered using the words *equality* and *fraternity* but decided they were too controversial, since many people opposed equal rights for women and blacks.

When I sing our national anthem, "The Star-Spangled Banner," I must confess to some conflict within, because it is a war song; nevertheless, I do sing. On the other hand, I sing with enthusiasm "God Bless America," for it is my prayer for my country. Likewise, having been in several countries around the world, I sing with conviction the song I have always thought should be the national anthem: "America the Beautiful."

My conditioning from my earliest existence taught me to resist, rebel, and mistrust. Consequently, when Barack Obama stood with his right hand raised in front of Chief Justice Roberts, and Michelle Obama held the Holy Bible on which his left hand rested, I wept for my ancestors and cheered for America — for the first time in my life. I want to be a part now. It feels good to say, "I pledge allegiance to the flag of the United States of America, and to the republic for which it stands, one nation, under God, indivisible, with liberty and justice for *all.*"

Pride Cometh

For sure, liberty and justice for all has been a dream deferred. But all things considered, no one can doubt that we have come a mighty long ways. Pride mounts for Americans, both black and white, as together we push the envelope of change. Never have we felt the hope we feel today.

Before I go further in this chapter, I feel I must digress for a moment. I supported and voted for Barack Obama for president of the United States, as I'm sure you've figured out by now. But I know that raises certain questions in the minds of many readers. More than once I've been asked, "How could you vote for someone who is pro-choice and a supporter of gay rights?" I ask you to consider my thoughts with an open mind.

The black experience is unique and driven by conditions that produce and influence core values as unique as the differences between blacks and whites. At some point, whites must resist the temptation to judge others by their standards or impose their values without considering the unique differences. It is my personal belief that abortion and gay rights, though sinful choices, are private moral issues. It is the church's responsibility to win the hearts and minds through conversion—not through the ballot.

The majority of black Christians do not believe in abortion or gay rights, just like the majority of white Christians. But here the paths diverge. Black Christians tend not to be one- or two-issue voters. To many of us, economic issues, young people dying in wars that should never have been fought, and disproportionate deaths as a result of poor or nonexistent health care all outweigh the *private* matters of abortion and gay rights.

To many whites, on the other hand, one's position on these two issues is the litmus test for suitability for public office. I will not attempt to persuade anyone from his or her privately held opinion on these matters; I only ask that you realize that it is about a difference of opinions in a pluralistic society.

Now, let's get back to the story of the 2008 election. Reactions came in from all over the world regarding the feelings provoked by Barack Obama's candidacy and election as president of the United States. Some of the comments could be instructive as we struggle to relate to the sentiments of minority cultures. The *L.A. Times* ran this article two days after the end of the 2008 Democratic Party primaries:

> **Obama's win brings hope and excitement to U.S.**
>
> **"I never thought I'd live to see this day," an 80-year-old supporter says, reflecting on the black experience in America.**
>
> By Bob Drogin, Erika Hayasaki and Robin Abcarian, *Los Angeles Times* staff writers
>
> June 5, 2008
>
> Until now it has been the stuff of fiction. But on Wednesday, Americans reckoned

with the reality: A black man is now a major party's candidate for president.

"I never thought I'd live to see this day," said retired pharmacist Arthur Dees, 80, marveling at Barack Obama's triumph. Dees, an Army veteran, recalled that he attended Dwight D. Eisenhower's inauguration in 1953, but was not welcome in any downtown Washington hotel or restaurant. "They were all segregated," he said, as he shopped at a mall in Wheaton, Md., a blue-collar community 12 miles north of the White House. Fighting back tears, he added, "My people have always had doggone names. We were darkies. Then colored. Next they called us Negroes. After that, we were black. Now, we're Afro-Americans. But with Obama, we're going to be just Americans. Won't that be something!"

"... So Help Me, God"

Until the 2008 race-transcending Iowa primary victory, made possible by a 96 percent white population, I was not proud to be an American for reasons already stated. But when Barack Obama, his wife, Michelle, and their two daughters came to the stage to hail their Iowa victory and receive the thunderous applause of excited white Iowans, I wept and said quietly, "America, all is forgiven." Then I and millions of others, black, brown, and white, rolled up our sleeves and said, "Okay, it's on now."

Every black American has a story of how that moment made them feel. It was visceral and vindicating. It was a deep and personal victory. Likewise, every black American, as well as many, many Americans of every race and nationality, wept openly on Thursday night, August 28, 2008, as Barack and Michelle Obama mounted the stage in Denver, CO. to the tumultuous cheers of one of the greatest political gatherings in political history, they accepted the nomination of the Democratic Party for president of the United States of America.

As powerful as that night was, it was exceeded by yet another historically awesome moment. That moment, the most thrilling moment of my life, came Tuesday, November 4, 2008, after the polls closed in California and CNN announced, "CNN is prepared to project Barack Obama as the next president of the United States of America." There are no words to describe the joy.

I was in York, Pennsylvania, having helped my son Michael, a paid campaign worker, man the phones and get out the vote. At the election-night returns party, I was surrounded by whites from all over the country and around the world who had worked very hard and now were nervously watching with us as the returns came in. When the victory announcement was made, the standing-room-only crowd erupted with earsplitting screams, yells, hoots, and hollers. I will never forget that feeling or the sights and sounds of that moment.

Complete strangers hugged and kissed me and said, "Congratulations. God bless America!" I saw an elderly black man leaning against a wall, shaking his head in disbelief and weeping big tears. For black America, this was unmistakably the proudest moment in the history of the United States of America. For millions and millions of African Americans, we will say this, by far, was our proud-to-be-American moment. It was the night our dungeon shook and our chains fell off. It was the night we became full citizens. It was the night that changed our history, altered our self-esteem, and made us feel like we finally belonged. It was a night that removed stigma, gave us new standing in the world, and changed forever the way our children would view themselves. In a moment; in the twinkling of an eye – we were born again.

Barack Obama embodied the best black Americans had to offer. If he was not viewed as a viable, eligible, worthy candidate, then it seemed to many that there would be no hope for equality in America. Likewise, on the night of November 4, 2008, the white American electorate embodied the best America had to offer. The powerful and the privileged, the dominant culture and the majority race, with imperfect understanding but hope for a more perfect union, went behind the curtain and pulled the lever for change.

With the whole world watching, white men and white women voted in overwhelming numbers to unlock the chains and break the curse. In state after state, city and suburb, North and South, they stood in long lines and with their votes removed a stigma and turned a page. The majority ruled in favor of a minority, and men and women in their sixties collapsed in tears and disbelief that they had lived long enough to hear freedom ring.

In addition to that cold Iowa night, the warm and beautiful night in Denver, and the rainy, cool autumn evening on Tuesday, November 4, 2008, there was one last magic moment that trumped all previous moments. I was privileged to be a part of that history in the making. With more than two million other people, I stood in the Washington Mall in front of the Capitol in the midst of the largest crowd I had ever seen. Many more people spilled into surrounding streets for two square miles, and hundreds of millions more sat in front of televisions around the world to bear witness to what is now fondly called "the Moment." It was the moment that fulfilled the 1963 prophecy of Dr. Martin Luther King Jr. in his famous "I have a dream" speech:

> This will be the day when all of God's children will be able to sing with new meaning, "My country 'tis of thee, sweet land of liberty, of thee I sing. Land where my fathers died, land of the pilgrim's pride, from every mountainside, let freedom ring."

> And if America is to be a great nation, this must become true. So let freedom ring from the prodigious hilltops of New Hampshire. Let freedom ring from the mighty mountains of New

York. Let freedom ring from the heightening Alleghenies of Pennsylvania. Let freedom ring from the snow-capped Rockies of Colorado. Let freedom ring from the curvaceous slopes of California.

But not only that: Let freedom ring from Stone Mountain of Georgia. Let freedom ring from Lookout Mountain of Tennessee. Let freedom ring from every hill and molehill of Mississippi. From every mountainside, let freedom ring.

And when this happens, when we allow freedom to ring, when we let it ring from every village and every hamlet, from every state and every city, we will be able to speed up that day when all of God's children, black men and white men, Jews and Gentiles, Protestants and Catholics, will be able to join hands and sing in the words of the old Negro spiritual, "Free at last! Free at last! Thank God Almighty, we are free at last!"

Barack Obama, a black American, an African American, a colored man, a Negro man, stood steady in front of the world with right hand raised and uttered the final words of the historic moment that changed the world: "So help me, God." With that, everybody around me yelled and cheered wildly again and again. I cried and cried and cried. A white lady and her husband hugged me tightly and rubbed my back until my uncontrollable sobs had ceased. I shouted as loudly as I could: "It's done! It's done! It's over! It's over! Praise God! Praise God!" I tell you unequivocally, this was the proudest moment of my life, and for the first time, I was proud to be American.

Discussion Guide

1. Define patriotism.

2. Discuss the irony of Native American "patriotism."

3. Where do double standards come from? Describe your double-standard experience.

4. Where were you and what were your first thoughts concerning "the Moment"?

Chapter 9

PHYSICIAN, HEAL THYSELF

I was sitting in the reception room of a doctor's office recently when suddenly the double doors swung open and the doctor walked in, stopping at the nurse's desk to give her a record and some faintly audible instructions. The five people in the room waiting with me all looked up at the same time then looked at one another. The doctor's arm was in a sling.

Of course, none of us knew why the good doctor's arm was in a sling, but I could tell by the expression on each face that each person was thinking, *If he's messed up, how can he help me?* I immediately thought of the Scripture in Luke 4:23: "Physician, heal thyself" (KJV).

The church finds itself in just such a situation—it is the physician with a broken arm. Before the president-elect could even be sworn in, a battle was already raging between the church and homosexuals who disagreed with the president-elect's choice of who would lead the prayer of consecration at the presidential inauguration.

Too often the church finds itself in the thankless position of building bridges and fences at the same time. Combine that with its history of missed opportunities to preserve life and stand up for the disenfranchised, and one can understand the charge "physician, heal thyself."

For sure, the church's dilemma of whether to love and license or curse and confront is real and serious. Paradoxically, the same politics that elected the first black president also rejected, on the same day, the sanctioning of gay marriage in California's Proposition 8. Go figure.

Even when the church must speak out against the lifestyle of those they seek to save, they must also humbly discriminate between human rights and social rights, even as they close their eyes and grit their teeth to the charge "physician, heal thyself." So let's get at it. Let's take a look at religion in general and the Christian church in particular. Let's examine cause and effect as it relates to the graying of our message in the church and in the world. Let's admit that we truly must bring order to our own house first. Let's humbly share with one another what the world already knows: that we do not have all the answers. But we do know the one who does — the omniscient Jehovah.

We must confess that our fractured religious institutions are not houses of perfection, nor are they houses of ill repute. They are human institutions first; therefore, they are flawed in their understanding of how to implement what we think we know about God. Our pursuit of God is full of tragic misrepresentations of

Him, and we have committed horrible crimes against one another in the form of ethnic cleansings, religious persecutions and inquisitions, human enslavement, and discrimination based on race, gender, caste, class, and money.

Maybe the most difficult part of this introspection is coming to the realization that it is too complicated to ever untangle the origins, histories, cultures, and politics of our religious beliefs. The final admission needs to be that only God can straighten out this mess. And lest we become victims of the paralysis of analysis, we must take the Word and get on with the business of living life until we die. In the meantime, we must deal with the scourge of racism in our histories, our politics, and our religion.

Discussion Guide

1. Identify at least four church catch-22s (building bridges and fences at the same time).

2. How should the church deal with its lack of self-esteem?

3. In what ways are the church's moral positions outdated?

4. How is it possible to embrace the sinner without embracing the sin?

Chapter 10

RACE-BASED RELIGION

It seems to me a natural consequence that earthly majorities foster diseases such as racism and sexism. Whether the power to impose one's will comes from numbers, as in a vote, or from weapons of war, the effect is the same: the majority rules.

In his book *PowerNomics,* Dr. Claud Anderson defines racism as "the exercise, the use, and the granting of power, privilege, and advantage based on race." *(PowerNomics: The National Plan To Empower Black America; by Claude Anderson ED.D; 2001; Bethesda, MD.; pg.5)* There is no sin in choosing your own kind. The sin comes when you choose your own kind at the expense of the other kind. In other words, when privilege is extended selectively with favor for one's own race it is, by definition, racist.

When such a circumstance has existed for centuries and with the blessing of constitutional law, racism becomes the national legacy. Only a counterinsurgent institution such as the church can mount a sustained challenge to it — unless the church has been co-opted by the secular system. Sadly, that is exactly what has happened in our nation. The church has become entangled and influenced by a secular political majority. The church's converts are all too often co-opted by politics and reconverted by lifeless religion. These religious zealots carry over the habits and proclivities of a worldly past, ironically becoming the very thing they preach against.

The fragmented church adopts myopic issues concerning its denominations and doctrines at the expense of the human relationships so important to Jesus, the founding head. We would rather win the vote to shut down a liquor store on Sunday than be accused of being a friend to sinners, or worse yet, a liberal compromiser. As the great philosopher of the comic strip Pogo once mused, "We have met the enemy, and he is us."

The church has the power to change the world, but it has instead been changed by the world and adopted a "world" view as opposed to a "kingdom of God" view. Mixing politics with Christianity, some Christians now find themselves in the peculiar position of supporting the invasion of a country suspected of harboring weapons of mass destruction — weapons, I might add, that never materialized. Consequently, we are still entangled in a war that much of the world believes to be wrong — a war that has cost both the country and the church its moral authority. The church, in bed with the world, has lost both its voice and its moral authority to effect change.

This entanglement with the world is historical and long-standing. In early church history, emperors such as Constantine corrupted the church's purity, doctrine, and message by declaring Christianity the state religion and thereby secularizing a religious institution. This compromising entanglement lived on and was seen in recent history when the Ku Klux Klan, the official terrorists of the South, based its murderous acts on Scripture and received spiritual cover from mainline denominations in the South. The signature symbol of the Ku Klux Klan, a burning cross, is the most cherished icon of Christianity; yet, the burning of crosses often preceded Klan-led lynchings, bombings, and shootings of other Christians whose only crime was being black.

One of the largest and fastest growing denominations in the world recently came to some stunning conclusions followed by even more startling confessions:

> Acknowledging that their repentance came 30 years too late, leaders of 21 white Pentecostal groups gathered in Memphis to close the racial rift with their African-American brethren...

> ..."Racism in the Pentecostal-charismatic community must be eradicated," B. E. Underwood, head of the Pentecostal Holiness denomination, declared as the conference opened. "What a difference it would have made during the civil rights movement in America if all

the children of the Pentecostal revival had stood together," Underwood said.

Throughout the meetings, sponsored by the 46-year-old Pentecostal Fellowship of North America (PFNA), white leaders expressed regrets that their history has been tainted by openly racist attitudes. One historian, Cecil Robeck of Fuller Theological Seminary, presented a 71-page paper describing, among other prejudices, how an Assemblies of God presbyter justified segregation in the South by teaching that God intended the races to live separately. The "father of American Pentecostalism," Charles Parham, continued to endorse the Ku Klux Klan as late as 1927, Robeck said. [*PENTECOSTALS RENOUNCE RACISM*; By Lee Grady; *Christianity Today Magazine*; December 12, 1994; Vol.38 No.14]

The church must deal with racism head-on, or racism will continue to mock and undermine the key tenets of Christian faith. We must work with terms that define racism from the perspective of the victims. But before we can deal with racism, we must see it in its wider context as the sin of exclusion and division that is also manifested in sexism, classism, and denominationalism. These are quadruple manifestations of the same monster spirit of division and cannot be defeated solely by human intellect, politics, or traditional religion.

The supernatural concept of Christian unity and reconciliation is advocated in the most important prayer Jesus ever prayed (John 17), and it is the most important assignment ever given to believers (2 Cor. 5:16–21). It is also the antidote prescribed by God to defeat the four-headed foe of racism, sexism, classism, and denominationalism.

Jesus made the strategy for winning hearts and minds clear when He said:

> The goal is for all of them to become one heart and mind—just as you, Father, are in me and I in you, so they might be one heart and mind with us. Then the world might believe that you, in fact, sent me. The same glory you gave me, I gave them, so they'll be as unified and together as we are—I in them and you in me. Then they'll be mature in this oneness, and give the godless world evidence that you've sent me and loved them in the same way you've loved me. Father, I want those you gave me to be with me, right where I am, so they can see my glory, the splendor you gave me, having loved me long before there ever was a world.
>
> —John 17:21–24 MSG

This scriptural passage is called Jesus' high priestly prayer and is considered by many to be the most important prayer in the New Testament. It is unmistakable in its attempt to set both tone and strategy for this new concept called "the church."

As strategic as John 17 is, the apostle Paul kicks the doors of the church wide open with his blockbuster statement that tears down walls both within and without the church. This passage is the litmus test for whether any congregation is a legitimate New Testament church. It gives the church its assignment in the world and sets forth the concept that, if applied, has the potential to destroy divisions of all kinds, both ancient and modern:

> Because of this decision we don't evaluate people by what they have or how they look. We looked at the Messiah that way once and got it all wrong, as you know. We certainly don't look at him that way anymore. Now we look inside, and what we see is that anyone united with the Messiah gets a fresh start, is created new. The old life is gone; a new life burgeons! Look at it! All this comes from the God who settled the relationship between us and him, and then called us to settle our relationships with each other. God put the world square with himself through the Messiah, giving the world a fresh start by offering forgiveness of sins. God has given us the task of telling everyone what he is doing. We're Christ's representatives. God uses us to persuade men and women to drop their differences and enter into God's work of making things right between them. We're speaking for Christ himself now: Become friends with God; he's already a friend with you. How? you ask. In Christ. God put the wrong on him

who never did anything wrong, so we could be put right with God.

— 2 Corinthians 5:16–21 MSG

The ministry of reconciliation as presented in the above passage is a clear and precise word of instruction and direction for the church. In my opinion, it is the perfect antidote for racism and denominationalism.

Furthermore, this passage makes it perfectly clear whose responsibility it is to cure society of these treacherous diseases. It is the responsibility of the church—not the government—therefore, the church must not rely on remedies from the Supreme Court or a local community coalition to combat these moral issues. Some, but not all, moral issues do become social issues, but this fact only emphasizes the need for preventive intervention by the church before that happens. When the church weighs in after the fact, it is a messier fight.

Racism finds cover when it is practiced in the church. Hitler was able to thrive in the moral void created by the silence of Christians throughout Europe. In the United States, racism found cover in the South because most white churches either forbade or discouraged blacks from attending their worship services. Some Southern churches even harbored racist members of the terrorist Ku Klux Klan.

In 1995, the Southern Baptist denomination made an extraordinary move to confess and repent of the slavery and racism that was the foundation of its existence:

A century and a half after its founding in Augusta, Ga., the Southern Baptist Convention appears ready to mark its sesquicentennial with a historic—and controversial—admission: The denomination was founded on proslavery sentiments in the turbulent period leading up to the Civil War. Three separate resolutions will be delivered to the SBC's annual meeting in Atlanta, beginning June 20, that acknowledge that Northern and Southern Baptists split in 1845 because Southerners allowed missionaries to own slaves, a practice Northerners repudiated.

Also at the meeting, Southern Baptist leaders are expected to repent of modern-day racism and ask forgiveness of African-Americans.

"We felt that it is just totally inappropriate for us to come to Atlanta to celebrate our heritage and our past without dealing with this dirty linen in the closet," Richard Land, executive director of the denomination's Christian Life Commission, said of the move to repudiate the SBC's proslavery history. "If we want to celebrate our past with a clear conscience, we need to deal with the negative aspects of our past in a proactive and a redemptive way," added Land, who helped draft one of the resolutions.

The SBC's efforts reflect a broader trend among religious groups. More and more, denominations are seeking to atone for historical sins, from the

Evangelical Lutheran Church in America repudiating the anti-Semitism of Lutheranism's Martin Luther, to a broad range of churches disavowing the subjugation of American Indians by European explorers. (Adelle M. Banks, *National Catholic Reporter*, June 16, 1995)

White Pentecostals and charismatics have become very sensitive and, more important, very proactive in establishing forums of opportunity to reverse the curse of racism among Christians. Jack Hayford, whom I love and often refer to as the Pentecostal Billy Graham, responded to the question, what do you understand racism to be? His answer was telling and instructive to blacks like me who are inclined to commit the same sin of insensitivity we accuse whites of:

It is very difficult to use the term "racist" or "racism" with people that love the Lord and who tend to be agreeable to all peoples without making them feel as though you have just slapped them in the face. What I have tried to do is establish a climate in which people can, with perception, say, "Oh, I do need to repent." Intentionality is the key word for the living church today, and that goes for all points on the color spectrum. That is not just a white responsibility. All of us have a responsibility to exercise intentionality, and it begins with recognizing that there is more than I can imagine that I don't recognize. I need to say first, "Holy Spirit, would you show me what I don't see, and what I do see, would you help me to act on it when I see it?" [*An Interview With Jack Hayford; by Dr. Cecil M. Robeck; PCCNA Reconciliation; Summer, 1998; pg.12*]

Only as I engage my intentionality am I, a black man, able to resist the instinctive response to Hayford's very first sentence. I could easily take issue with it, but the premise grabs me. "What I have tried to do is establish a climate in which people can, with perception, say, 'Oh, I do need to repent.' " That statement makes me put my gun back in the holster. I realize this is a respected white leader talking to another white leader about white people. His goal or his premise is larger than my taking exception. He is telling me, if I can hear him, how to talk to whites if I want change.

The point is, tolerant dialogue — listening to each other with patient ears and an open discussion where all guns (tongues that shoot down the other person's truth) are checked at the door — can lead different-color brothers where both want to go.

Discussion Guide

1. Define racism from your perspective. Define it from the perspective of your other-race friend.

2. How is the church racially compromised? What is the fix? How can it "uncompromise" itself?

3. What can be gained by unconditional listening? What are the hazards?

4. Do you think that biblical reconciliation as described in 2 Corinthians 5:16–21 is as key as the author suggests? Why or why not?

Chapter 11

ORDER IN THE HOUSE

Ephesians 4:11–13 sets the backdrop for this chapter: "It was he who gave some to be apostles, others to be prophets, others to be evangelists, others to be pastors and teachers. He did this to prepare all God's people for the work of Christian service, in order to build up the body of Christ. And so we shall all come together to that oneness in our faith, and in our knowledge of the Son of God we shall become mature people, reaching to the very height of Christ's full stature." [GNT] Let's look at the implications of this Scripture in greater detail.

Apostolic Restoration and Its Impact on Race and Reconciliation

Since the mid-1990s, the movement towards the restoration of the fivefold ministry gifts of Ephesians 4:11, sometimes referred to as the apostolic restoration movement, has exploded in numbers and influence. It is a movement that reflects the church's attempt to return to charismatic government or, said another way, Spirit of God– led government.

As usual, the theologians and doctrinaire types will be debating the legitimacy of the movement for some time to come. However, when we put all such moves or movements in historical perspective, this fresh interest in the fivefold ministry seems to be a kind of millennial correction whose mission is to bring revival of purpose and dynamic effectiveness as it reestablishes order in God's kingdom on the earth.

It is perhaps the contemporary use of the term *apostolic* that creates the most discussion in these latter days. The biblical title *apostle* is defined from the original Greek word *apostolos*, which literally means "to send away," or "one sent on a mission," as defined by *Merriam-Webster's Collegiate Dictionary,* Eleventh Edition. In its earliest usage, it had a more political or even militaristic application, as in one sent by the king or general to bring order to a conquered territory. The one sent was the king's "apostle" and his mission was "apostolic."

Over time, this term and others, such as *bishop* or *prophet,* evolved (some might even say "mutated") to include an expanded meaning and importance that accommodates the contemporary religious trend of our time. This has resulted in new and contemporary uses of the term *apostle* that are close to the original meanings that existed in the first few centuries after Jesus' ascension.

Harold W. Boyer, in his book *The Apostolic Church and the Apostasy*, writes, "Actually, when we use the term 'apostolic,' we mean that which was taught and established by the apostles" (p. 10). While I concur with Dr. Boyer, I would take it one very important step further. When we use the term *apostle* today, we usually use it in the context of Ephesians 4:11, not merely as a reference to what the twelve original apostles taught and established. We are saying that these powerful ministry gifts never ceased and therefore continue today through the men and women that God has gifted to be apostles, prophets, teachers, pastors, and evangelists.

Consequently, when I use the terms *apostle* and *apostolic* in this chapter, I am referring to the men and women called by God to minister and sent by God to establish order and government in the territory that belongs to God; namely, His church, or His kingdom.

The apostle, for those who ascribe to the fivefold ministry model, is the highest leader in the New Testament church, according to Ephesians 4:11. When I use the term *apostolic restoration*, I am referring to the spiritual move that seems to be spreading among churches and across denominational lines that seeks to restore the Ephesians 4:11 ministry model to the body of Christ.

The apostles and prophets of the early church exercised power and authority that brought order, peace, and direction to the body during troubled times. For example, they moved quickly to heal a widening rift between the Grecian Jews and the Hebraic Jews when the Grecian Jews noticed their widows were being overlooked in the daily distribution of food. A careful selection of seven Spirit-filled men who were full of wisdom and faith solved the problem so completely that the entire group was satisfied, both Greek and Hebrew. "So the word of God spread. The number of disciples in Jerusalem increased rapidly, and a large number of priests became obedient to the faith" (Acts 6:7).

This was the New Testament church in its pure yet developing form. Its government was both apostolic and charismatic in that the apostles selected, authorized, and sent seven Spirit-filled men with gifts of wisdom and faith. We must not miss this point: in the kingdom of God, no other version of government is authorized and empowered to solve problems or do conflict resolution except this version that many now call "apostolic government."

This presupposes two things. First, wherever there are human beings, there will be problems and conflicts of one kind or another; and second, a system and strategy created in the omniscient wisdom of God Himself has been provided to handle all problems and conflicts whenever and wherever they occur.

Order in God's house is a prerequisite to the house's authority to bring order to the world that it is assigned to flavor and influence. We have religious or racial chaos or order in direct proportion to the establishment of divine order in the earth. When we attempt to confront the spirit of division without flowing in divine order, we operate as a handicapped society and as the body of Christ suffering from denominationalism and sectarianism, even as the world suffers from the diseases of racism, bigotry, and prejudice from the same spirit.

Unity and agreement in the kingdom of God, therefore, are not options — they are imperatives. Unity and agreement are spiritual antidotes for spiritual and social ills and are the fundamental answer for every issue. God knew the issues that would arise. He also knew that the issues in the world would find their way into the church as men and women, who themselves are in process, transition from the world to the new community that is the church.

Thus, the problem of racism and denominationalism has had a solution from before the foundation of the world. The church's government is based on spiritual unity, spiritual agreement, and spiritual authority exercised under the auspices of apostolic, Spirit-filled leadership as demonstrated in the New Testament book of Acts, sometimes referred to as the Acts of the *Apostles.* This threefold apostolic framework of spiritual unity, agreement, and authority maintains the church's peace and mission within the church and without.

The Holy Scriptures note the interesting case of Nicolas, a Greek convert from Antioch who converted to Judaism. As a Grecian-Jewish-Christian full of faith and the Holy Spirit, he was selected to be one of the first deacons in the early church. He was an international, interfaith, interracial phenomenon. He truly embodied the spirit of the New Testament Church (see Acts 6:5–7).

When Cornelius, a godly captain of the Roman Guard, was instructed in a vision to send for Peter, God had to put Spirit-filled Simon Peter into a Spirit-induced coma before he would carry the gospel to this Italian soldier. It is almost comical. This was post-Pentecost, but Spirit-filled Peter still had racial issues. Peter was operating from an old segregationist paradigm inherited from his secularized Jewish upbringing, but God was out to break it once and for all under the new order — the new covenant of the kingdom of God.

As Peter entered the house of Cornelius, his opening words to the gathered crowd struck a death blow to racism and segregation based on religious background or nationality. In Acts 10:27–29, he boldly announced, "You know, I'm sure that this is highly irregular. Jews just don't do this — visit and relax with people of another race. But God has just shown me that no race is better than any other. So the minute I was sent for, I came, no questions asked" (MSG). Peter further confessed in verses 34 and 35, "I now realize how true it is that God does not show favoritism, but accepts men from every nation who fear Him and do what is right" (NASB).

Peter's opening testimony was not enough. It required God's official signature and seal of approval, so in verse 44 the Bible says, "No sooner were these words out of Peter's mouth than the Holy Spirit came upon the listeners. The believing Jews who had come with Peter couldn't believe it, couldn't believe that the gift of the Holy Spirit was poured out on 'outsider' Gentiles, but there it was—they heard them speaking in tongues, heard them praising God" (MSG).

Is this it? Is this the New Testament model? Is this the answer for the terrible problem of racism that we have suffered from for centuries? Is it as simple as "visit and relax with people of another race" and share the outpouring of the Holy Spirit? Yes, it really is!

No Difference Between Them and Us

If we fail to see the outcome of all this Holy Spirit interaction in the book sometimes called the Acts of the Apostles, we will miss the whole point and purpose of apostolic leadership. The new church leaders—apostles, prophets, bishops, pastors . . . whoever or whatever you want to call your leaders—understood the importance of order and agreement. They made decisions that ensured the developing church would be grace based, not race based.

When Peter arrived in Jerusalem for the "first annual ministers' conference," he was questioned about his race mixing. According to what is known as "the law of first mention," we must examine the first mention of a word, doctrine, or concept in the Bible if we hope to properly understand it. Therefore, we would do well to pay close attention to the evolving government and the mention of titles, methods, and the use and delegation of authority.

The apostle Peter defended his ministry of inclusion to the Gentiles by rehearsing his encounter with God in a vision. He shared with the brethren:

> And as I began to speak, the Holy Ghost fell on them, as on us at the beginning. Then remembered I the word of the Lord, how that he said, John indeed baptized with water; but ye shall be baptized with the Holy Ghost. Forasmuch then as God gave them the like gift as he did unto us, who believed on the Lord Jesus Christ; what was I that I could withstand God? When they heard these things, they held their peace, and glorified God, saying, Then hath God also to the Gentiles granted repentance unto life.

> — Acts 11:15–18 KJV

Case closed — racism and denominationalism solved! Hold on — that's not quite the whole story. This was the first hearing of this word. As we have learned in the real world and throughout Scripture, old traditions die hard and require that we listen until we hear. We just don't seem to get it from one sermon only.

In the fifteenth chapter of Acts, the question arose from the old conservative Jewish believers, who were determined to conserve their cultural and racial identity and purity, about whether the new Gentile converts should be circumcised. Peter again rehearsed his experience:

When there had been much disputing, Peter rose up [someone must always stand up and proclaim the latest truth to combat the zeal of one who is steeped only in the latest tradition] and said unto them, Men and brethren, ye know how that a good while ago God made choice among us, that the Gentiles by my mouth should hear the word of the gospel, and believe. And God which knoweth the hearts, bare them witness, giving them the Holy Ghost, *even as he did unto us;* and put no difference between us and them, purifying their hearts by faith. Now therefore why tempt ye God, to put a yoke upon the neck of the disciples, which neither our fathers nor we were able to bear?

— Acts 15:7–10 KJV, emphasis added

The newborn Pharisaic Jewish believers were still being emptied of their prejudices. Old habits and old sacred traditions die hard, but die they must.

Peter's testimony was witnessed by Barnabas and Paul (v. 12). After Barnabas and Paul spoke, the leading apostle, James, said, "Men and brethren, hearken unto me. . . . Wherefore my sentence is that we trouble not them, which from among the Gentiles are turned to God: But that we write unto them, that they abstain from pollutions of idols, and from fornication, and from things strangled, and from blood" (Acts 15:13, 19–20 KJV).

Please note the authority and leadership exercised: "My sentence is . . ." There was one voice, one instruction, and one direction given by one person. Today in many contemporary denominations, churches give such a leader who operates in this gift the biblical title of "bishop" or "apostle." What is clear, however, is that James's authority was not in the title, but in his anointing to lead and the Jerusalem council's anointing to be submitted to his apostolic leadership.

What follows next in the Scriptures is equally revealing. After the apostle said, "My sentence is . . .," verse 22 says, "Then pleased it the apostles and elders, with the whole church, to send chosen men of their own company to Antioch with Paul and Barnabas; namely, Judas surnamed Barsabas, and Silas, chief men among the brethren" (KJV). James did not operate as a lone ranger. In spite of his awesome power and authority, he was submitted to the power of agreement: "Then pleased it the apostles and elders, with the whole church . . ."

The lesson of submission and the grace of humility are often learned in the crucible of trial and trouble; nevertheless, they are prerequisites to professional and public success in ministry. Perhaps the greatest lesson I have ever learned in my forty-plus years of ministry is the submission of individual authority and leadership to the agreement of the apostles, overseers, elders, and the entire church. Submission to authority greater than oneself is a biblical imperative.

Here is a true confession: in direct proportion to my submission to my bishop, apostle, or elders was

I successful. In those seasons of my ministry where I failed to be submitted, my success was limited and short-lived. The sooner the church returns to the admonition of 1 Thessalonians 5:12–13, the sooner the restoration of order in God's house will come: "Now we ask you, brothers, to respect those who work hard among you, who are over you in the Lord and who admonish you. Hold them in the highest regard in love because of their work. Live in peace with each other."

The final word that went out from the Jerusalem council was this: "It seemed good unto us, being assembled with one accord, to send chosen men unto you with our beloved Barnabas and Paul, men that have hazarded their lives for the name of our Lord Jesus Christ. . . . For it seemed good to the Holy Ghost and to us, to lay upon you no greater burden than these necessary things" (Acts 15:25–26, 28 KJV).

The Holy God has made it clear: He is not a respecter of persons. God does not regard color, race, gender, ethnicity, nationality, or religious history, "but accepts men from every nation who fear Him and do what is right" (Acts 10:35). If you want favor from God, fear Him and do what is right. Even when His methods change, the sovereign and immutable God does not change His principles.

The churches that get it (I discuss this in chapter 20) have all found that their success in growing multiracial and multicultural fellowships comes from apostolic intentionality. By this I mean Spirit-filled and Spirit-sent leadership that orders the intentional "visiting and relaxing with other races" in order to unlearn or reprogram the new citizens of the new kingdom.

Apostles, bishops, overseers, pastors — whatever name you give them — must themselves be thoroughly convicted that the Bible is the rule of faith, that Christ alone is Lord, and that we are all equal in His sight when we obey His Word. These ministry leaders must order the kingdom by creating the forums and atmospheres that nurture an other worldly "comm-unity." They, the apostolic leadership of the body, must authorize Spirit-filled preachers to preach it, Spirit-filled teachers to teach it, and Spirit-filled deacons to practice the administration of love and care without respect to race, religious background, gender, culture, or nationality. Only the theocratic reign of the Creator's government, which is the rule of the kingdom of God in the hearts of men and which influences the political systems of this world, has the credibility and moral authority to handle that relentless nemesis of humankind — racism.

According to the Holy Scriptures, such a kingdom was established on the day of Pentecost (Acts 2). No one had ever seen anything like what happened on that day. No wonder Jesus had told the disciples to wait in Jerusalem until "the promise" came. This promise was the enabling power of the new kingdom, a kingdom that would be led by supernaturally enabled leaders called apostles, prophets, evangelists, pastors, and teachers. Each of these callings would have unique and specialized abilities to order the kingdom. Their authority would not come from a vote or a government of the people, by the people, and for the people. Their authority would come from their demonstration of Spirit and power (1 Cor. 2:4).

Discussion Guide

1. Discuss whether apostolic order as recorded in Ephesians 4:11 is a biblical principle or a command. Explain your choice.

2. What is the connection between racial reconciliation and the apostolic order sometimes referred to as the fivefold ministry gifts?

3. Who are the strong religious leaders, Christian or otherwise, who have significant political impact in our country or in our world today?

4. Discuss and distinguish between Christianity as a political kingdom and Christianity as a kingdom that influences politics.

Chapter 12

THE PHENOMENON OF REVOLUTION

On January 12, 2009, the *Barna Update* made a shocking statement: "The survey shows half of Americans believe the Christian faith no longer has a lock on people's hearts. Overall, 50% of the adults interviewed agreed that Christianity is no longer the faith that Americans automatically accept as their personal faith, while just 44% disagreed and 6% were not sure." While the issue of unity is one that haunts the church world in general, according to this national survey, Christianity is no longer America's default faith.

Many church leaders concur with the findings of George Barna as reported in his book *Revolution*. He asserts that today's denominations and religious reformations have become irrelevant as a world force and have lost the moral authority and credibility to effect serious change. In regards to racial reconciliation, it is all too true. Too many churches continue to play word games and pose for token photo opportunities during fifth-Sunday unity celebrations that present them with a false public persona.

I have experienced firsthand some of this disturbing trend. In 2004, a denominational leader I worked with confided in me that he could not move too fast towards racial reconciliation for fear that those leaders he depended upon for financial support would revolt and withhold their money. He advocated instead a ten-year plan that involved focus groups, studies, consultants, committees of professors, and handpicked "leaders" to "guide the process." At best, his efforts could be viewed as mere window dressing; at worst, a bureaucratic filibuster. He did admit, however, that in ten years he would be long retired, and the process would be left to the next generation.

During that time span, we took pictures together, and when his regional conference rolled around, he paraded us in front of his peers and superiors as silent icons of racial reconciliation. It may have looked good on the outside, but it was obvious to us all that not only did the plan lack integrity, but also the leader lacked commitment. It was not enough that the plan was disingenuous; to make matters worse, it was put forth by a denomination whose chief tenet is the unity of all believers.

Today the gifted young men and women of such organizations barely pay lip service to these groups, rarely attend their functions, and have quietly and independently moved on, joining what Barna calls "the revolution." Indeed, the church that is now evolving out of this ecclesiastical revolution is not your grandma's church, content to march in lockstep to the drumbeat of tradition on the path of least resistance. The high and lofty proclamations of past generations of spiritual leaders have finally come full circle and are now being inspected by a new, socially sensitive generation that has little use for the rhetoric of ancient denominational idealisms.

As denominations position themselves to be minimally offensive to constituencies that send big checks, those same denominations move farther and farther from the liberating truths that founded them. That some still argue the various faces of unity after a hundred or more years of claiming it as the cornerstone reason for existence is tragic.

The church today has aligned itself with religious extremists who work hard in the name of Jesus to kill by war what they cannot convert by witness. Whatever strategy we have for transforming the gay community or winning to Christ the pregnant woman seeking an abortion is lost in the street fights and angry debates that alienate both groups and polarize the country. The church, too impotent to heal the disease, shoots the patient.

In a day when every Sunday should be a celebration of growth and a demonstration of kingdom dominion on earth as it is in heaven, some still argue and divide the body of Christ over doctrine and the traditions of man (see Colossians 2). While we should be plotting the expansion of the kingdom across denominational lines, we are instead fighting to limit it to those who maintain our particular traditions. Some denominations are even busy plotting to keep *believers* with different manifestations of the same spiritual gifts from being credentialed, while supporting racial intolerance and refusing to embrace racial diversity except under ideal laboratory conditions. All this goes on in the name of the Savior as the weary, cynical world goes to hell in a handbasket.

Whether you have wine at communion or at dinner — read my lips — I don't care! What I do care about is getting Don, my heroin-addicted friend, delivered from heroin and into the arms of the Savoir — and I really don't care about the order. Please forgive my tone; I am wiping tears as I write. I am remembering how sick my own priorities were until I met someone who needed God so badly that I was forced to drop all my concerns about dress standards, church protocols, traditions, rules, and regulations and rush him to the emergency room of God's love. To this day, I have trouble forgiving myself for being so stupid, self-righteous, and arrogant. In the silence of my personal introspection, I say to God, "Lord, I'm so sorry."

The love I have for fallen humanity came only after I quietly crashed and burned but experienced a patient Father picking me up and covering me with His love. Herein lies the key that initiates lasting change: repentance. "If my people who are called by my name will humble themselves and pray and seek my face and turn from their wicked ways then will I hear from heaven and will forgive their sins and will heal their land" (2 Chron. 7:14).

Then, I was intolerant of sinners who couldn't get it together, but today, I walk in His holiness—not my own. Now I'm intolerant of irrelevant religion and churches whose end product is an entertaining preacher or choir rather than the primary cause of the kingdom: the redemption of souls and the transformation of lives and lifestyles. Thank God for a growing number of churches that have tired of the game and are seeking hard after God, His presence, and His purpose!

There is now a growing number of pastors and congregations who are opting out of the ongoing argument over doctrines and traditions. Believing that agreement is the place of power, they have quietly and peacefully formed fellowships committed to the practice of functional and purposeful unity as well as to a full New Testament gospel. To do so, they have had to shake off the dark and haunting warnings of apostasy, backsliding, and worldly compromise.

According to pollster George Barna, who has dedicated his entire book entitled *Revolution* to this twenty-first-century phenomenon, there are many who no longer value church tradition and denominational organization. He says:

> As we travel together, I want to show you what our research has uncovered regarding a growing sub-nation of people, already well over 20 million

strong, who are what we call revolutionaries. What "established systems" are they seeking to "overthrow or repudiate" and "thoroughly replace," in Webster's words? They have no use for churches that play religious games, whether those games are worship services that drone on without the presence of God or ministry programs that bear no spiritual fruit. Revolutionaries eschew ministries that compromise or soft sell our sinful nature to expand organizational turf. (George Barna, *Revolution*, p. 13)

My own experience as a former General Overseer of a religious denomination concurs with Barna's findings. Many churches large and small have opted out and no longer concern themselves with the irrelevant goals of their denominational headquarters. Pastors of small, medium, large, and mega churches alike confess their weariness of political feuding, power struggles, and the worship of denominational heritage and history. They have disengaged from its politics and policies and have adopted new methods and names that distance them from any association with their dysfunctional religious past. Desiring to experience God up close and personal, they have shed the ball and chain of corporate headquarters in exchange for the fresh, real-time move of the Holy Spirit. They have embraced the joy and thrill of interacting in supernatural enterprises and engaging in spiritual warfare in order to follow the Spirit's lead rather than the dry, dead dictates of sterile committees or the petty politics of self-serving boards and councils.

There is evidence this phenomenon is happening at all levels—locally, nationally, and internationally—and among all races and denominations. The office headquarters of many denominations are experiencing a declining attendance in sanctioned conferences and in effect and influence over their pastors and congregations. God's people are hungering for revival, not recycled rhetoric, and they yearn to reflect the heart of the heavenly Father, not the traditions of their denomination's founding fathers.

"Jesus is the answer" can be a trite religious cliché or the key to unlock and unleash the will of God on earth as it is in heaven. Jesus really is the answer because He is the chief cornerstone of the church, which is the physical manifestation of God's kingdom on earth. And the answer to the world's issues is found in God's church, established on the day of Pentecost with the coming of His Holy Spirit.

The coming of the Holy Spirit marked the primary difference between the Old and New Testament people of God. The Holy Spirit empowers and enables the present-day church to operate by theocratic rule. In other words, God rules by way of His Spirit. He gives gifts to men and women to enable them to operate in the kingdom, carry out His kingdom agenda, and execute His kingdom strategy for taking and exercising dominion.

The only way the church can function successfully as the kingdom of God is to operate under the authority of the Spirit of God. It can thus be said that the kingdom of God is an army of Spirit-filled (God-influenced) and Spirit-controlled (God-controlled) men and women. They constitute the body of Christ, and the collective, or universal, body of Christ—red, yellow, black, brown, and white—constitutes the kingdom of God.

The church is a world inside of the world. The church is the place we come as worldly prodigals coming home to the Father by way of the new birth. We come out of the world to come into the church. In fact, the word *church* is derived from the Greek word *ecclesia,* which means "to come out of" or "the called out." The problem is, it is one thing to get a person out of the world, but it is another mission to get the world out of the person.

"And You Shall Have Power After . . ."

The grand strategy for these come-outers includes a new paradigm in governance. The kingdom of God, or the church of God, is governed by the gifts of the Holy Spirit of God that enable everyday men and women to overcome sin—every sin. These sins include but are not limited to those manifestations from the demon spirit of division, the father of racism, denominationalism, sexism, and classism.

The distinction between church and world is powerful and imperative and must be maintained if it is to be a moral compass on the earth. Either the church is a moral and spiritual compass for God, or it is simply one among many competing and collaborating religious institutions attempting to accomplish humanly what can only be accomplished supernaturally. God is more than a mascot of religion—He is the master of universal destiny and purpose.

The truth is, we cannot handle the complexities of racial and ethnic diversity without the help of God. This fact is made clear in Acts 1:8: "But you will receive power when the Holy Spirit comes on you; and you will be my witnesses in Jerusalem, and in all Judea and Samaria, and to the ends of the earth." For the body of Christ to operate multiculturally and internationally, the Holy Spirit must rest, rule, and abide in it.

As simple as this may sound, it is not always so simple to live out. It took divine revelation for Simon Peter to be delivered from his cultural and religious bias: "I now realize how true it is that God does not show favorites" (Acts 10:34 KJV). It is absolutely significant that the standard used to validate the new Gentile converts was the outpouring of the Holy Spirit on them in the exact same way that He had been poured out on the Jewish Christians. The power of the Holy Spirit was given to all equally, and Jesus' prophecy that they would be enabled to be worldwide witnesses was fulfilled.

When the Jewish Christians heard that Peter had gone among uncircumcised men, they where upset. Bigotry and ignorance among Spirit-filled Christian Jews was real and unvarnished. But God intended the young church to learn the crucial truth that He does not have favorites.

What evidence did Peter present to his fellow Jews? He said, "Before I'd spoken half a dozen sentences, the Holy Spirit fell on them just as he did on us the first time. I remembered Jesus' words: 'John baptized with water; you will be baptized with the Holy Ghost.' So I ask you: If God gave the same exact gift to them as to us when we believed in the Master Jesus Christ, how could I object to God?" (Acts 11:15-17 MSG).

And then comes the stunning revelation that changed everything: "Hearing it all laid out like that, they quieted down. And then as it sank in, they started praising God. 'It's really happened! God has broken through to the other nations, opened them up to life!' " (Acts 11:18 MSG).

The church is an organism — not brick and mortar, but lively stones linked and given relationship to God through His Holy Spirit. Without this relationship, we are blind to spiritual truths. Without this live link, we are powerless to effect change. Our authority, power, and life actually come from another world.

Our moral standards are not determined by who has the money, the military, or the vote. Our ability to let go of ignorance and prejudice is dependent upon our eyes coming open: "as it sank in." In other words, we have to see that we need to let it go. For us, it is not about the advantage we have because of numbers, for the church of the new paradigm will almost always be a numerical minority, but a power majority.

In too many cases, God's grand strategy for saving His creation has been all but neutralized by the very spirit of division it is commissioned to defeat. Eleven o'clock on Sunday morning remains the most racially segregated hour of the week. Somehow we have failed to recognize and overcome that spirit of division that exploits, disenfranchises, and divides the human race into polarizing classifications such as majorities, minorities, classes, denominations, and other divisive designations.

When Jesus announced the Year of Jubilee, that every-fifty-year celebration when slaves were freed, debts forgiven, and mortgaged family property returned, He was actually defining the ultimate purpose of the kingdom of God under the new covenant, or new paradigm. He declared, "God's Spirit is on me; he's chosen me to preach the message of good news to the poor, sent me to announce pardon to prisoners and recovery of sight to the blind, to set the burdened and battered free, to announce, 'This is God's year to act!' " (Luke 4:18 MSG).

The Message of Hope

As the famed newscaster Walter Cronkite used to say, "And there you have it." Could anything be clearer? Luke 4:18 is the agenda spoken from the Master's mouth. Let's break it down and see what it means.

1. "God's Spirit is on me": Make sure God's Spirit is on you.

2. "He's chosen me to preach": You are called and chosen by God Himself to speak up.

3. "To preach the message of good news": Whatever you preach, make sure it's *good* news. Telling a pregnant woman seeking an abortion that she is going to wake up in hell is *not* good news. Telling that same pregnant woman that God loves her and her baby and has an awesome plan for both of them and that you and your organization will help take care of her and her baby *is* good news.

4. "To the poor . . . to prisoners . . . to the blind": Go to these people; they are your primary mission.

5. "Set the burdened and battered free": Go free the burdened and battered from what burdens and batters them.

He laid it out! Don't lobby Congress about Mary the prostitute. But if you do, be sure to lobby about Sam the john, as well. Say to her accusers, "Back off. He that is without sin, let him cast the first stone." As far as Mary the prostitute goes, cover her and tell her the good news that there is no one accusing her, including you. Tell her that Daddy (her heavenly Father) sent you to tell her to come home; He's not mad, and He's not holding anything against her (see 2 Corinthians 5:19).

Then take her to a safe place, feed her, clothe her, find her children, and work with her until you get her delivered from her bondage. Tend to her bruises, train her, and rejoice with her when she pours expensive perfume over her Savior's head and dries it with her hair—and no wisecracks.

Our hope is our message, and our message is unconditional love and liberation. As we distance ourselves from that message, we will find ourselves mired in the mud of spiritual confusion, compromise, and contradiction. When that happens, the place meant for healing begins incubating the virus that Jude spoke about in his exhortation to the first-century Christians. His words are as true today as they were then:

> Our spiritual communities are as susceptible to disease as our physical bodies. But it is easier to detect whatever is wrong in our stomachs and lungs than in our worship and witness. When our physical bodies are sick or damaged, the pain calls our attention to it, and we do something quick. But a dangerous, even deadly, virus in our spiritual communities can go undetected for a long time.

> Dear friends, I've dropped everything to write you about this life of salvation that we have in common. I have to write insisting—begging— that you fight with everything you have in you for this faith entrusted to us as a gift to guard and cherish. What has happened is that some people have infiltrated our ranks (our Scriptures warned us this would happen), who beneath their pious skin are shameless scoundrels.

—Jude 1–4 MSG

The kingdom of God is the greatest threat to evil and the greatest hope for the victims of evil. And let me say it here: we are all victims of the evil one. He is not trying to injure us; he is trying to kill us all so as to rob God of His glory—redeemed humanity!

Whether we are members of the majority race or a minority race, we are all victims. We are all wounded by fiery darts from without (Satan) and friendly fire from within (the church), but the fight "ain't" over! We have a promise from God signed in blood that upon this rock (Jesus) He will build His church, and the gates of hell *shall not prevail!*

Discussion Guide

1. In what ways has the church lost some of its moral authority? How can it be restored?

2. What can the church do to restore its credibility?

3. How does the Bible address racism? Does God tolerate racism in the believer? What is the biblical response to racism?

4. What is good news to the poor? What kinds of things does it encompass?

Chapter 13

SHOOTING THE WOUNDED

Sinner Bashing

It has often been said that the Christian army is the only army that shoots its wounded. There is, unfortunately, much truth to that. The most ardent antiabortion crowds are often composed of mean-looking, mean-acting "Christian" people taunting and shouting insults, and threatening and committing acts of violence and even murder— all in the matchless name of Jesus. Typically, the crowd is white, suburban, conservative Republicans who know nothing about the young women having the abortions or the doctors and nurses performing the procedures. They do not live or worship in the neighborhood among those most likely to seek services from a public clinic.

On the other hand, we have laissez-faire liberals who would offer Satan himself sanctuary in the name of a grace that has no victory and a Jesus who doesn't require change. These liberal extremists are clouds without rain, offering a delusional promise with no real substance.

In the heated battles that we face in a pluralistic society, it is important to keep the battle lines clear so that we do not shoot those who are already wounded. I trained as a medic in the U.S Army during the Vietnam War. My job was not to question the wounded, except to find the source of any bleeding and stop it, but to minister healing. Interestingly, we medics were trained to help anyone we found on the battlefield, including the enemy.

In spiritual warfare, we must distinguish between the enemy and the enemy's victim. We must be careful not to throw the baby out with the dirty bath water. In particular, the hot-button issues of abortion and gay rights create much havoc and confusion on the battlefield. These issues remind me of a sign posted in the entrance of our mess hall in Vietnam. The sign read, "Know Your Enemy!" and showed a North Vietnamese soldier in uniform. But the problem was, the ones killing us were not the North Vietnamese as much as it was the Viet Cong, the enemy that lived among us, wearing civilian clothes and looking just like the peace-loving South Vietnamese.

Today we fight issues, such as abortion and gay rights, that are the issues of everyday people. Some of those struggling are your relatives, neighbors, and friends. Some of these everyday people you know and interact with daily, and some you do not. The problem is, sinners don't wear uniforms that identify them according to their sin. They are just like you and me in every way. Our individual issues may differ, but not by much.

"Be not deceived: neither fornicators, nor idolaters, nor adulterers, nor effeminate, nor abusers of themselves with mankind, nor thieves, nor covetous, nor drunkards, nor revilers, nor extortioners, shall inherit the kingdom of God. And such were some of you: but ye are washed, but ye are sanctified, but ye are justified in the name of the Lord Jesus and by the Spirit of our God" (1 Cor. 6:9–11 KJV). That list includes a broad spectrum of sin, and most of us could see ourselves in at least one of those areas. But the point is, we are all drowning in sin until we allow Jesus, the lifeguard, to rescue us. Once He pulls us out of the water, He won't leave us until he gets the water out of us.

Proverbs 11:30 says, "He that winneth souls is wise" (KJV). In these last days, we are in great need of wisdom as we face the many women and men caught in the act of sin, whether great or small. Our challenge is to respond like Jesus, without respect of person or of the sin—"for such were some of you." According to the law, the woman caught in the act of adultery should have been stoned, but Jesus' response was to cover her by challenging her accusers: "He that is without sin among you, let him first cast a stone at her" (John 8:7 KJV). Jesus' response should be our example and the classic response of those who are called by His name.

Once again, however, the public reputation of too many Christians is more like the ancient Pharisees and less like the timeless Christ Jesus. We are more ready to stone in judgment than to cover with mercy. It is as if we believe we are kingdom police called to arrest, judge, and execute those who break the law. But the Bible says that God extends mercy to those who give mercy in place of judgment.

In discussing gay rights, I contend that the homosexual individual is not the enemy—the lifestyle is. I believe the church must not treat homosexuals any differently from the way Jesus treated the woman at the well, the woman caught in the act of adultery, or Peter after he denied Him. Satan is the enemy—not the homosexual.

It is a contradiction in terms and behavior to love someone whose *human* (and even religious) rights I am trying to deny. Kill the disease—not the patient. Although as a Christian I resist the gay agenda becoming public policy, I also resist public policy bringing undue harm to gays personally. My experience is that love wins every time. Thank God for the grace that enabled me to come into my purpose, and thank God for the people of God who patiently and sometimes impatiently suffered my failures and mistakes until that grace kicked in and I finally got it!

I refuse to substitute a worldly remedy for the spiritual remedy, lest I inadvertently give power to the state to force everyone to become Christian, which was the heresy of Constantine. I find it absolutely wonderful that I am free to follow Christ, but I am equally free to not follow Him. I live in a country where I don't have to be a Christian. It is a matter of my free choice and free will.

I am able to live with men and women of other races, religions, and relationships, and that is wonderful. To not allow others to peacefully coexist with me because they do not believe what I believe is religious bigotry of the highest order and does not bring honor to God. God is not diminished by the existence of one who does not believe in Him. He loves broken humanity so much that He died for all of us before we as yet knew Him: "But God demonstrates his own love for us in this: While we were still sinners, Christ died for us" (Rom. 5:8).

There is no racism and bigotry worse than that practiced in the name of Jesus and that seeks to find its authorization in Scripture. It is time that we pick the fight with Satan—not his victim. Let us become more proactive and less reactive when dealing with those whose beliefs are opposed to our faith. That is what I have decided to do.

When I get the opportunity to vote on public policy, I will promote and vote my faith, but I will not let Satan cast me as the enemy of sinners. I am not worried about being politically correct. I am concerned about being biblically correct, about being God's friend, as was Abraham. Jesus did not demonstrate against the clubs where sinners hung out drinking, but rather He hung out with them so much that others called Him a friend of sinners. When was the last time you were honored with that description?

On the other hand, to peacefully coexist with competing lifestyles is a great opportunity to "prove what is the good, perfect and acceptable will of God" (Rom. 12:2). Many of us were once in the same condition as those we are ready to stone. Many of us have relatives and friends who are looking for the Jesus who will cover the "caught"—not expose them and hold them up to ridicule.

Every day I knowingly and unknowingly tolerate the excesses of people all around me who will go to hell, not because they were sinners, but because they knowingly rejected the remedy for sin. Said another way, they refused the medication. Should we who have been healed of the disease of sin spend our time stoning the diseased, or should we spend it convincing them to take the meds?

For example, I am free not to be gay. The gay individual is free not to be straight. Why not have a contest and let the God who answers by fire be God? In other words, let's see if the demonstration of power and Spirit will win my gay friend to the Lord, which, after all, is my goal; or let's see if my gay friend's lifestyle will win out. Let us not lose sight of the goal, which is souls—changed hearts, minds, and lives. Votes, guns, money, and legislation cannot win or save a single soul; only the Spirit of God can do that.

A few years ago, a friend who worked for one of the airlines called me and said, "The airline I work for has decided to stop discriminating against us single employees. They changed their benefit policy from giving free flying privileges only to spouses to allowing anyone the employee chooses to have the same benefit. They no longer punish us for being single. Since you travel a lot, I thought you might be able to use this benefit."

For about one year, I flew first class virtually free because of this individual's generosity and her employer's policy. Many churches were blessed because they did not have to pay for my transportation. Should she have been denied the right to give that benefit to a married man? To a boyfriend? To a girlfriend? Should anyone care? Why should we make dark, speculative judgments about the nature of the gift or the relationship?

My point, albeit somewhat tortured, is this: it is not a battle worth fighting over, particularly as it relates to gay rights. It is a human right. I do not lose anything by allowing a human benefit to go to another human being. In fact, I may win a friend. The church is called to transform the world by the renewing of minds, not by denying human rights, winning arguments, or impeding another person's adult freedoms.

Jesus stopped the ones who were willing to stone a woman to death in order to fulfill their inhumane and bogus religious law. We can do no less. By the way, the institution of marriage was in trouble long before gays came out of the closet and wanted to be recognized.

Is our goal to push them back into the closet? Unless the gay person chooses to go straight, what difference will you have made with your angry rhetoric and self-righteous judgments? Absolutely none! Put the stones away.

I have concluded that I would rather have mud on my face for extending mercy than blood on my hands for rendering judgment. The body of Christ has been duped into winning battles and losing wars. The enemy has succeeded in dividing us over hot-button issues and distracting us from doing what we do best: sharing the love of a very good God.

The church is at its best when it pursues its scripturally mandated purpose to "speak up for the people who have no voice, for the rights of all the down-and-outers. Speak out for justice! Stand up for the poor and destitute" (Prov. 31:9 MSG). That is its message of hope, and therein lies its power.

Discussion Guide

1. Describe the natural conflicts that arise in religious states with multiple religions.

2. Have you ever won a gay brother or sister to Christ? If so, how did you do it? If not, how would you go about it?

3. Discuss the potential for religion in general and Christianity in particular to be tyrannical.

4. In the case of the woman caught in adultery, was Jesus wrong for not enforcing the law? Why or why not?

PART 3

STRATEGIES AND APPLICATIONS

Chapter 14

BODY PARTS

I have said it already, and I will say it again and again from slightly different angles and contexts: I am offering the body of Christ as the ultimate answer with the ultimate strategy to cure what ails the world. I am suggesting that the church's mission as the representative of the kingdom of God on earth is also the answer to disease, poverty, and social dysfunction. What a claim!

Unfortunately, in the twenty-first century, it is better not to proclaim what one cannot demonstrate. The world has many choices and little tolerance for false advertising. Religious institutions as a whole are so splintered they have lost credibility and influence. In Christianity alone, the spectrum of religious belief stretches from the sublime to the ridiculous, with every denomination attempting to carve out a place in the hearts and minds of prospective believers.

Given this sad history and the resulting weakness that haunts all religion today, it is absolutely imperative for the Christian church to renounce its divisions and the spirit that has caused them and embrace in its place a broad revival of unity and inclusiveness. The church's unity is its strength. It is precisely why we are exhorted to endeavor to keep it (Eph. 4:3).

We are parts of a whole. The American Baptist Association is only a *part* of the body of Christ. The Roman Catholic Church is only a *part* of the body of Christ. The Hispanic Concilio is only a *part* of the body of Christ. The Native American Association is only a *part* of the body of Christ. And whatever part you belong to, no matter how large or small, never forget that you are not *it*. You are just a *part* of it—got it? As your mother might say, "Now go somewhere and sit down, and just be glad you're in!"

I thank God for you. I bless God that we are family. It is so good to be home. It is wonderful to know that none of us are orphans. One glorious day, my Daddy sent word through my older Brother, "Come on home. Daddy is not mad at you."

No, for real, read the will: "God was in Christ reconciling the world to himself, not counting men's sins against them" (2 Cor. 5:17–19). Now if God is not counting sins, what are you staring at? If God is not counting our sins, then do you think He really cares that much about my theology or yours? Then why all the arguing and division?

The unity of the New Testament church of God will not be achieved through the "man rule" of conferences, caucuses, or focus groups. Unity in the church will be achieved only as we return to "God rule." Thus, we must focus less on our intentional political structure and more on initiating intentional revival forums that can inspire a fresh hope and directly influence the communities in which we live. The world is waiting for a healthy, relevant church to get busy with its divine business.

Intellectualism cannot lead us into repentance, love, or interracial unity. Unity and reconciliation in all forms must come from within the heart, and that is the exclusive domain of the Spirit. When we encounter the Spirit of God, the same Spirit that brooded upon the waters during creation broods upon our intellects and hearts, forging us into new creatures and empowering us to act like it. Only then can we become the physical representation of God's kingdom on earth. We are fraudulent counterfeits when we try to represent God as fractured, faction-filled, politically correct religious organizations.

Unity is not the end; it is the means to the end. It cannot be faked or staged. We do not have it because we visit or meet each other once a year, dim the lights, and light a few candles while softly singing, "Kumbaya, my Lord, kumbaya." We have unity only when we *dwell* together. As the psalmist says, "Behold, how good and how pleasant it is for brethren to dwell together in unity" (Ps. 133:1 KJV). Verse three of that same chapter says, "It is there [in unity] that God commands blessing, even eternal life." [KJV]

Additionally, we do not have unity if we achieve reconciliation inside our own denomination but fail to achieve it with denominations that may not look like us or share the same doctrinal emphasis, but who, nonetheless, preach Jesus and pursue His lifestyle to the best of their understanding. God calls all believers everywhere to be one. Could the denominational divisions we experience in the kingdom of God be a root cause of the alleged irrelevance of the traditional church?

In George Barna's book *Revolution,* he states: "Whether you want to or not, you will have to take a stand in regard to the revolution. It is on track to become the most significant recalibration of the American Christian body in more than a century" (George Barna, *Revolution,* p. ix). Revolution is inevitable when the status quo is unbearable.

The church today suffers the same rate of disease, death, divorce, violence against women, and racial strife as does the world outside it. But far too often we receive communion every first Sunday in a warm, fuzzy-feeling ceremony with little regard to the biblical warning found in 1 Corinthians 11:27–30: "Therefore, whoever eats the bread or drinks the cup of the Lord in an unworthy manner will be guilty of sinning against the body and blood of the Lord. A man ought to examine himself before he eats of the bread and drinks of the cup. For anyone who eats and drinks without recognizing the body of the Lord eats and drinks judgment on himself. That is why many among you are weak and sick, and a number of you have fallen asleep." Are we guilty of not "recognizing the body of the Lord"? It may be a more serious matter than we think.

We are left with very specific and clear instructions on how to discern the body:

> You can easily enough see how this kind of thing works by looking no further than your own body. Your body has many parts — limbs, organs, cells — but no matter how many parts you can name, you're still one body. It's exactly the same with Christ. By means of his one Spirit, we all said good-bye to our partial and piecemeal lives. We each used to independently call our own shots, but then we entered into a large and integrated life in which he has the final say in everything. (This is what we proclaimed in word and action when we were baptized.) Each of us is now a part of his resurrection body, refreshed and sustained at one fountain — his Spirit — where we all come to drink. The old labels we once used to identify ourselves — labels like Jew or Greek, slave or free — are no longer useful. We need something larger, more comprehensive.

> —1 Corinthians 12:12–14 MSG

As Christians we are at once new creatures and a new race. It may be time for every denomination and reformation movement to redefine Christian unity and rededicate themselves to reflect the wider, more comprehensive view promoted by the New Testament, which also includes gender (Gal. 3:8) and denominational unity (1 Cor.1:11–13).

I prophesy to you, to those who hold out for denominational or reformational distinctives, you will be irrelevant and obsolete in five years. The time has come to discern the body. The reality is, like many of you, I was born, raised, and born again in a denomination that departed from its original emphasis on unity as blacks began to invade its ranks. It wasn't long before its denominational and reformational identity became the organization's greatest pride and priority. As pride replaced purpose, the founders of this reformation were not merely honored, but hallowed—even above Scripture itself. Its truth was no longer progressive and revelational, but fixed, finite and finished.

Our reform movements are fast becoming irrelevant monuments. After all these years, we all must admit that our particular group is not the whole; that the inception of our organization did not launch the reincarnation of the New Testament church; that we are a part of the broader church, and even our part has parts. The true church is still the called-out of God, who, though scattered in many different folds, still constitute the body of Christ.

The question remains, is it a contradiction to be denominationally divided but racially united? Is it possible to be united denominationally but divided racially? Both divisions are ludicrous, sinful, shameful hypocrisies not worthy of our Savior's blood sacrifice.

Christian Unity

Christian unity includes *all* Christians everywhere. We are one church, and only God has the membership book. When we divide over detailed doctrinal interpretations, we further damage that unity and make it more difficult for the world to believe that God has sent Jesus (John 17:21). In fact, it is nothing more than pride that gives us the audacious nerve to think that we have the right, power, or intelligence to determine who is right and who is wrong, who is in and who is out.

God moved Paul to write one of the most powerful statements in all of Scripture concerning this aspect of Christian unity:

Welcome with open arms fellow believers who don't see things the way you do. And don't jump all over them every time they do or say something you don't agree with—even when it seems that they are strong on opinions but weak in the faith department. Remember, they have their own history to deal with. Treat them gently.

For instance, a person who has been around for a while might well be convinced that he can eat anything on the table, while another, with a different background, might assume all Christians should be vegetarians and eat accordingly. But since both are guests at Christ's table, wouldn't it be terribly rude if they fell to criticizing what the other ate or didn't eat? God, after all, invited them both to the table. Do you have any business crossing people off the guest list or interfering with God's welcome? If there are corrections to be made or manners to be learned, God can handle that without your help.

—Romans 14:1–4 MSG

This passage always reminds me of a verse in a familiar hymn from my childhood. Called "Reformation Glory," the words read:

> Christians all should dwell together in the bonds of peace,
> All the clashing of opinions, all the strife should cease;
> Let divisions be forsaken, all the holy join in one,
> And the will of God in all be done.
> (Charles Naylor, "The Reformation Glory," from the
> Hymnal of the Church of God, 1922, p. 421)

If we do not broaden our definition or standard of Christian unity, we will become increasingly alienated from one another within the local fellowship, our national church organizations, and the universal body of Christ. The reality is, we are already there. Indeed, for the past several centuries, petty disagreements have divided churches and created entire religious movements.

Twenty-five years ago, for example, I used to preach against Christian women wearing jewelry. I preached it as worldly and contrary to the standards of Bible holiness. It was the way I had been taught. One day my sixteen-year-old daughter said, "Daddy, I have always believed what you preached. If you tell me that I will go to hell for wearing earrings, I will not wear them, nor will I ever raise the question again."

I said, "Sweetheart, in good conscience, I can't tell you that you will go to hell, but . . ."

Carmen interrupted me, "If I won't go to hell, then would you let me decide?"

That day I celebrated my own deliverance and bought my daughter a pair of pearl earrings. This rather simple experience forced me to deal with the broader question of integrity, inclusion, and acceptance. It forced me to deal with my inclination to protect a tradition in the face of the preponderance of scriptural evidence and, more important, to know the difference. If I was to have scriptural integrity, I had to dump my pride and back down.

Living with Diversity

Now my point is, if we believe that God has more sheep than those in our small fold, and if we believe that Baptist, Methodist, Apostolic, Pentecostal Assemblies of the World, Church of God in Christ, Church of God (Anderson, Indiana), Church of God (Cleveland, Tennessee), and Church of God Holiness believers are also in the New Testament church, then on what basis do we deny either fellowship or cooperative evangelistic ventures? Is it simply because they are not called by our denominational name or that they cherish a different doctrinal emphasis?

Do you really believe that I will go to hell because I speak with other tongues, call myself or someone else bishop, do not practice the washing of feet, and enjoy listening to secular love songs? If you don't really believe that, then what's the point? Why do we judge one another so? Is it that you don't mind my being in heaven with you, but you just don't want to worship with me here on earth? Okay, we can do that, if you want.

If, for example, I speak with other tongues, I can join a fellowship where I can practice my gift among others who believe the same thing. Likewise, if you don't accept this practice, you can join with others who share that belief. But if you discover this gift while a member of a traditional church that doesn't believe in it, don't try to convert everybody around you to your point of view. That will only cause confusion and division. Confusion is not of God, and He hates division; so just go on over to the Full Gospel church to worship God and speak in tongues all you want.

The point is, one size does not fit all. But "blessed are the peacemakers, for they shall be called the children of God." [Ma.5:9KJV] Now that fits all! Some of us have greater fellowship and cooperation with other denominations than we have with other churches and Christians in our own fellowship. Sadly, our traditions have become stronger than biblical truth as we continue to preach unity but practice division.

Jesus said in John 10:16, "You need to know that I have other sheep in addition to those that are in this pen. I need to gather and bring them too. They'll also recognize my voice. Then it will be one flock, one Shepherd" (MSG).

As Christians, we are commissioned to go into all the world. Jesus' final prayer in the New Testament was not intended for any one organization, whether white, black, Hispanic, Asian, Native American, or any other nationality or ethnicity. Jesus prayed on behalf of *all* believers and those who would believe in Him through the witness of the disciples. All means all. Jesus said:

> My prayer is not for them alone. I pray also for those who will believe in me through their message, that all of them may be one, Father, just as you are in me and I am in you. May they also be in us so that the *world* may believe that you have sent me. I have given them the glory that you gave me, that they may be one as we are one: I in them and you in me. May they be brought to complete unity to let the world know that you sent me and have loved them even as you have loved me.
>
> —John 17:20–23, emphasis added

In 2 Corinthians 5:17–20, the apostle Paul repeats the principle that God was in Christ reconciling the world to Himself, not counting men's sins against them *and* has committed to us the ministry of reconciliation. The entire marvelous notion is linked to verse 17, which says that this all begins when we become new creations in Christ.

If we put the two passages together, Jesus' prayer in John 17 and Paul's declaration in 2 Corinthians 5, we see the inescapable truth: the world cannot believe until and unless Christians are reconciled to God and to one another. As noted earlier, the psalmist says in this unity and reconciliation are found blessing and eternal life (Ps. 133:3).

Is it any wonder that so many Christian denominations today appear to be going in circles? As they practice their limited, private interpretations of Scripture and cling to their often prideful traditions that are so sacred to them, they become idols and objects of worship. Until we repent of our pride and the religious idolatry that excludes all who do not believe our particular doctrinal emphasis, until we get about the business of bringing souls to Christ and not just to our religious organizations, we will continue to experience spiritual decline, chaos, and irrelevance.

You may be experiencing just this scenario even as you read this book. Unfortunately, you may recognize yourself in the paragraphs above. Your church is either aging and dying for a reason, or it is growing and alive for a reason. But even if your church or denomination is experiencing spiritual decline, it does not have to continue. Thankfully, you are not without hope or remedy. Let me tell you what you can do.

No matter how bad the storm, stay in the ship! The ship of Zion shall sail and prevail. Jesus declared, "You are Peter, a rock. This is the rock on which I will put together my church, a church so expansive with energy that not even the gates of hell will be able to keep it out.

"And that's not all. You will have complete and free access to God's kingdom, keys to open any and every door: no more barriers between heaven and earth, earth and heaven. A yes on earth is yes in heaven. A no on earth is no in heaven" (Matt. 16:18–19 MSG).

God is at work in the earth through His church. Don't let the petty doctrinal squabbles, the lingering racial hang-ups, and the denominational divides fool you. There is an outpouring of His Holy Spirit going on at this very moment. Turn your cup up!

There are signs of revival, revolution, and restoration across the universal church. With just a few changes of attitude and perspective, your church can come alive, grow, and effect change in your community.

"A revolution is about changing what exists. Change requires leaders who intentionally introduce new direction" (George Barna, *Revolution*, p. 83). Across the globe powerful new leaders and powerful churches and parachurches are taking the kingdom by force. Many are loyal mainline denominational members. Others are independent breakaways from denominations that, in their view, stifled the revelation and move of God in them.

We are as diverse as we are black, brown, yellow, and white. I do not believe that diversity ends with race. I believe our views are as different as our educations, backgrounds, and temperaments. Yet I believe that each unique entity has specific purpose in the divine scheme. The conservatives, for instance, keep our feet to the fire and chastise our proclivity to wander too far off course. The liberals keep us compassionate and in touch with the heart of God. The moderates keep us balanced, sober, and away from either extreme.

When we read Scripture, we are compelled to believe that absolute agreement on every issue for the favor or purpose of God is *not* a prerequisite for effective ministry (and probably not possible). For example, in Acts 15:36–41, two superstar apostles clashed big time. In Acts 13:4, Scripture tells us that Paul and Barnabas were both sent forth by the Holy Spirit; nevertheless, we see in Acts 15 that these two Spirit-filled men of power had a knock-down, drag-out argument. In fact, the disagreement was so bad that they split up and went their separate ways.

Read it in Acts 15:39: "They had such a sharp disagreement that they parted company." The Message Bible says, "Tempers flared, and they ended up going their separate ways." The King James Version says, "And the contention was so sharp between them, that they departed asunder one from the other." But notice this: the Holy Spirit was with them before the split, and the Holy Spirit went with each of them after the split. So much for our either-or debates. By the way, the great apostle Paul was eventually reconciled to John Mark, the person over whom he and Barnabas separated.

You can draw your own conclusions, but it is clear to me that not all splits are bad. If we don't multiply, we *will* divide—but let the church roll on. "And we know all things work together for good to them that love God, to them who are the called according to his purpose" (Rom. 8:28). If God is in a thing, we will know it. Likewise, if God is not in it, we will know that too. Judge nothing before its time (1 Cor. 4:5).

We are all parts of one body that has many other parts. Just as the eye cells are specialized to create sight, the spiritual body is specialized to produce souls in the kingdom. Just as the foot is not required to be the eye, neither should we demand that our organizational detail be the same throughout the body. Though our parts specialize, we are most useful if and when we cooperate with one another.

Again, we are Apostolic, Church of God in Christ, Church of God, Baptist, Methodist, Catholic, Lutheran, Presbyterian, Episcopalian, Pentecostal, Charismatic, evangelical, and independent. From Joseph Garlington in Wilkinsburg, Pennsylvania; to T. D. Jakes in Dallas, Texas; to Rick Warren in Saddleback, California; to Joel Osteen in Houston, Texas; to Rick Hawkins in San Antonio, Texas; to Gilbert Thompson in Boston, Massachusetts; to Paul Sheppard in Palo Alto, California; to Tim Clarke in Columbus, Ohio; to the many great leaders across the length and breadth of this country— hearts and lives are being touched and changed through compelling worship and anointed preaching as diverse as the congregations they represent.

The global reach of great ministries across racial and denominational lines is unparalleled. An awesome demonstration of power and Spirit is breaking down racial, denominational, and gender barriers. Old men are dreaming dreams and talking in their sleep, confirming the Word and providing words of knowledge and wisdom to new warriors. Young sons are hearing the hearts of their fathers and having visions and building effective ministries, small, medium, mega, and mighty. A powerful anointing is being poured out on women, just as the prophet Joel prophesied. Cynthia James, Juanita Bynum, Paula White, Rita Johnson, Joyce Meyer, Jackie McCullough, Diana Swoope, Marilyn Hickey, and many other women of God have confounded the theologies of their critics as men and women fall in love with Jesus through their powerful ministries.

Joseph Garlington at Covenant Church of Pittsburgh, (located in Wilkinsburg, PA) Paul Sheppard at Abundant Life Fellowship in Palo Alto, and Rick Hawkins of Place for Life in San Antonio are shining twenty-first-century examples of the growing number of churches that have exploded the racial barriers. Families of every color and nationality flock into their sanctuaries, seeking the living God and singing and dancing in celebration of who God is and what He has done. As a result, the light is shining in darkness, and darkness is being dispelled.

Discussion Guide

1. How can Christian unity be accomplished in our time? To what degree, if any, is it possible to have unity between Christian and non-Christian religions?

2. According to Psalm 133, what is the importance of unity?

3. Is unity a principle or a fixed law? Explain.

4. What do you feel accounts for the growing trend towards multiracial congregations?

Chapter 15

UNITY AND COMMUNITY

In a quote most often attributed to American scholar Sam Pascoe, lies a stinging summary of the history of Christianity: "In the beginning the Church was a fellowship of men and women who centered their lives on the living Christ. They had a personal and vital relationship to the Lord. It transformed them and the world around them. Then the Church moved to Greece, and it became a philosophy. Later it moved to Rome, and it became an institution. Next it moved to Europe, and it became a culture. Finally it moved to America, and it became an enterprise. We've got far too many churches and so few fellowships." *[The Question That Changed My Life; David Ryser; The Peacebringer Musings; Posted July, 2009]* Sobering words indeed, but let's examine more closely the thought behind such a statement.

A Time to Scatter

I suppose we could discuss the issues of community in all its faces for a very long time. We could debate the secular definition given in *The American Heritage Dictionary*, Second College Edition: "a group of people living in the same locality and under the same government; a group or class having common interests." Or we could expound on the biblical principles that suggest relationship as the foundation of all community, with the family as community's first institution and the expansion of family relations into various and diverse groupings of tribes, clans, cultures, and races. From the biblical perspective, the split of the first family from their Father-Creator set off a chain reaction of further splits and splintering that assumed final form when man began his second attempt at independence in the building of the Tower of Babel.

The Bible says that at this time "the whole world had one language and a common speech" (Gen. 11:1). One language and a common speech seems to have given the people of the earth the key to unlimited potential and power to determine their own course and means of existence and, in fact, caused God to preempt a second attempt at self-determination. Genesis 11:5–9 reads:

> But the Lord came down to see the city and the tower that the men were building. The Lord said, "If as one people speaking the same language they have begun to do this, then nothing they plan to do will be impossible for them. Come let us go down and confuse their language so they will not understand each other." So the Lord scattered them from there over all the earth, and they stopped building the city. That is why it was

called Babel—because there the Lord confused the language of the whole world. From there the Lord scattered them over the face of the whole earth.

We are led to believe that mankind is only a shell of God's original intention. We are left to speculate what life might have been like without the sin of Adam and Eve. In this Genesis 11 passage, we are again left to wonder what God had in mind for the human race before preempting its second attempt to go it alone.

I come away from the reading of this passage with the distinct impression that unity and speaking the same language are principal prerequisites to a super-community where "nothing they plan to do will be impossible for them" (v. 6). These characteristics are apparently more powerful than we have yet imagined. And it should be noted that the principle of unity and community works no matter who works it.

More important, just as unity of language and plan made them a force that even God had to reckon with, division disrupted and diluted their potential, destroyed their plan, and scattered their community. Is it any wonder, then, that all throughout Scripture we see God's continued intervention in human affairs in order to bring reconciliation and the restoration of relationships?

Those who answer the call to be reconciled to the Father are known by several purpose-revealing terms, specifically *ecclesia*, the Greek term that means the "called out" from which we derive the English word *church*. Since the death and resurrection of Jesus Christ made this reconciliation available to all, we call this newly constituted family "the body of Christ." This explains the importance of 1 Corinthians 11:29's exhortation about discerning the body.

It is not coincidental that on the day the kingdom of God, or the church of God, or the body of Christ—whichever term you elect to use—was launched that an accompanying phenomenon occurred:

> When the day of Pentecost was fully come, they were all with one accord in one place. And suddenly there came a sound from heaven as of a rushing mighty wind, and it filled all the house where they were sitting. And there appeared unto them cloven tongues like as of fire, and it sat upon each of them. And they were all filled with the Holy Ghost, and began to speak with other tongues, as the Spirit gave them utterance. . . . And they were all amazed and marveled, saying one to another, Behold, are not all these which speak Galileans? And how hear we every man in our own tongue, wherein we were born?
>
> —Acts 2:1–4, 7–8 KJV

As God the Father and Creator of the universe moved to the last stage of His grand strategy to be reconciled to His family through righteous relationship, He did two very significant things: (1) He brought them together: "they were all with one accord in one place."

(2) He gave them one language: "And how hear we every man in our own tongue?" These divine prerequisites enabled the newly restored family to operate with God and one another through new supernatural tools of communication and power.

Unity and community, then, are not only the ends, but they are also the means. Clearly, the grand strategy of the kingdom of God is to gather out of the earth a people who will be reconciled to Him and to one another. The end goal is the restoration of God's family—the whole and entire body of Christ.

A Time to Gather

Nowhere does Scripture declare the whole body as a particular denomination or movement. The whole body is the whole of Christianity and includes *all* who have confessed with their mouths the Lord Jesus and have believed in their hearts that God has raised Him from the dead. (And I won't be mad if somebody gets into heaven with only that principle, but not that formula).

I repeat, some in the body are arms, and others are legs; still others are eyes, ears, or feet, but they all belong to one body. These body parts look nothing alike, but they are all in the body. Some are Baptist Christians, while others are Methodist Christians; still others are Church-of-God-Reformation-movement Christians, and some are Catholic Christians. But regardless of denomination, if they have accepted Jesus, they have been born into the kingdom and together constitute the whole body.

I believe that sometimes the form and method of accepting Jesus Christ as Lord and Savior may differ even within a particular Christian denomination. For instance, we have charismatic Catholics whose practices are not necessarily sanctioned by Rome. We have Full Gospel Baptists who are flat-out Pentecostal in what they believe and practice concerning the gifts of the Spirit as recorded in 1 Corinthians 11. In fact, so-called Pentecostalism has spread to most mainline denominations.

The point is, we can no longer be accurately classified by denominational pedigree. And who among us has been given that task anyway? There is a wonderful cross-pollination going on that confounds the purists and is revolutionizing previously held denominational stereotypes. Thank God, none of us will be at the pearly gates checking IDs. If I have believed on the Lord Jesus Christ, I shall be saved! Praise God! Yes, I personally might wince at someone's emphasis on the Virgin Mary, but if one accepts Mary's baby as Savior and Lord, he or she is my "blood" brother or sister; and in the words of the old saints, "Ain't nobody mad but the devil."

Come on, now — I mean, really — do you seriously believe that God has left my or your welfare and destiny in the hands of feuding theologians with their religious prejudices, private interpretations, and flawed conclusions? I don't think so! Isaiah said the way would be made so plain that the "wayfaring man, though a fool, would not err" (Is. 35:8 KJV). So give me a break! My opinion and your opinion notwithstanding will not change the fact that in the end, in heaven, there is going to be a number that no man can number. With that knowledge, I no longer carry the burden that the world will not be saved until it hears the Church-of-God-Reformation-movement version of the gospel.

Closing the Door After the Fly Is In

So, in practical, everyday, the-way-it-really-is terms, how shall we walk out this great definition of community; that is, "common units," people with common interests who live together? The Christian church is a community of Christian believers. If those Christian believers dwell in ethnically specific communities, we can logically expect their organizations and institutions to reflect the community's ethnicity. It might be called a kind of de facto ethnic concentration that is segregated by natural collection as opposed to natural selection. When de facto segregation exists, meaning segregation as a result of nonhostile circumstance as opposed to segregation imposed by law (de jure), how can Christians demonstrate kingdom-of-God unity?

First of all, I believe separation is a more accurate term than segregation in many cases. While the results, a monoethnic community, may be the same, the motive and spirit of such a community should not be prejudged.

Second, as Christians, we all must ask ourselves, what are we trying to do? What is our goal? Our goal is to represent the kingdom of God on the earth.

Third, if we agree with the goal, the issue becomes how best to represent God on this earth. I suggest the biblical strategy is unity, which is not only a winning strategy for the church but also a biblically prescribed antidote for the disease of racism.

The problem is, the body of Christ is so divided both racially and denominationally that it has neutralized its witness and made null and void its scriptural claims. The question at hand is, how do we unite? To what extent do we come together? Do we come together in spirit or in truth? In other words, do we come together in the spirit of program and ceremony, or do we actually join our purpose and our people? How do we close the door of ethnically exclusive fellowships in the same socially diverse community?

I am suggesting that the body of Christ must unite in spite of ethnicity, not according to ethnicity. I am suggesting it is inappropriate and ineffective to present the kingdom of God as single-race enclaves in multiracial communities, and I am further asserting that we are most effective when we dwell together in multiracial unity. Until we can completely eradicate the fly of division, we must cooperate as two or three until able to operate as one.

The temptation, however, is to give in to a kind of social and spiritual laziness and pretend we are united. We do this when we create artificial Kodak moments and staged unity events that are pitiful and impotent. In so doing, we actually surrender the power that comes from uniting.

The body of Christ attempts to assuage its conscience and excuse itself for not evangelizing cross-culturally. Such behavior, no matter how rationalized, sooner or later finds a silent sanction that leads to bolder steps of disunity and a widening of the breakdown as people flee their racially changing neighborhoods to live next door to their own kind. I completely understand the desire to live in a safer neighborhood and to maximize the value of property, but it seems to me that we concede territory when we base our actions on these types of motivations. Sooner or later, we will be forced to weaken our theology to adjust to our reality.

I question the absence of a sustained effort and the sincerity of any attempt to redeem the troublemakers and turn around communities in which we ourselves no longer live. In my humble opinion, it seems just a little disingenuous to move out of a community because of plummeting property values, in search of safer environments, or because the neighborhood is changing racially, then have yearly outreaches to those communities or stage "unity" Sundays to prove that we are interested in being multicultural. Such action, I think, reveals something about perceived value, if not spiritual integrity.

Regardless of personal motivation, we inevitably form committees and councils that racially represent our demographics. This means the black community will naturally form ministers' fellowships, credentialing committees, conferences, seminars, workshops, and conventions that are convenient and relevant to them because they live in a black community. Likewise, the Hispanic community develops concilios, credentialing processes, and conferences that are ethnically specific to them. This leads to a kind of de facto segregation, albeit innocent of ill intent.

Evolving out of all this is the reality of multiple conventions, credentialing committees, state assemblies, general assemblies, and ministers' fellowships. Sooner or later, someone comes up with the novel idea of, why don't we unite and come together as brethren and be one? After all, we are all Baptists or Pentecostals or whatever. Motivated by zeal, guilt, falling numbers, and loss of interest, the suggestion of a monthly, bimonthly, or annual joint fellowship is offered. Everybody thinks, why not? recognizing that they have a form but no power to change the community.

The question then becomes, who should dissolve their assets and organization for the sake of unity? If we overlook the fact that unity is a spirit that develops when we dwell together, we will only increase the problem by seeking artificial solutions. We will then come together in the name of a unity that does not change us or empower us to change others.

Here is an irony: in our coming together in such unity efforts, we gradually replace evangelistic dreams with look-busy programs as we gradually grow weaker and weaker. Not realizing our strength comes from united people around a shared purpose, we do not dwell together or create forums that seek to understand and celebrate our diversity. Instead, we quietly continue to abuse each other with self-serving, turf- protecting suggestions, offensive jokes, and status-quo plans that guarantee further negative attrition. Here's more irony: the more we meet, the faster we get nowhere.

But many pastors are realizing the fallacy of trying to sustain such fruitless efforts. In fact, a dear pastor-friend of mine just had his credentials withdrawn for not attending meetings just like these. What do you think happened to his congregation? It continued to thrive and grew exponentially. Of course, the pastor had to endure the rap that he was anti-unity and uncooperative. But I applaud him and others like him who are looking for likeminded pastors who want to truly dwell together — not perpetuate the sham of a false unity that exists on paper only.

Your Place or Mine?

When we arrive at the conclusion that unity means "united," "together," and "one unit," the merger of organizations and strategies for ecumenical evangelistic cooperation is inevitably suggested. But exactly how do we go about operating and cooperating as one after starting histories, leaving legacies, and indulging the specifics of our ethnicities for so long? Should we join together and operate as a new unit, or should we come together only for celebrations but operate separately?

Another question that must be answered deals with the very real issue of material possessions. Over the years, as denominations tended to the business of their particular visions, wealth was created and accumulated in the form of buildings, land, and various investments. If we join together, what do we do with our things, our "stuff"? What do we do with the properties and the treasuries of our separate organizations?

Who joins whom in this merger? Is it even possible to merge financial inheritance with racial heritages and histories that are, at best, estranged? How do we handle the obvious and not so obvious disparity of business and financial savvy and style? Should there be a requirement of material equality as a condition of equal enfranchisement?

These are all difficult yet relevant questions, and they have been much debated. But what happens most of the time is that the larger, older, and more financially stable group remains intact while the smaller group dissolves. This, however, may not be the best way, and numerous groups are breaking with this pattern in an effort to find a more harmonious solution to the problem. Let's look at one example.

Dr. Jack Hayford is the world-renowned senior pastor of Church on the Way in Van Nuys, California. Dr. Cecil Roebuck is a professor at Fuller Theological Seminary in Pasadena, California. Both men are members of the newly formed Pentecostal Charismatic Churches of North America, a newly formed group of black and white Pentecostals. Dr. Roebuck asked Dr. Hayford, "Why did the Pentecostal Fellowship of North America choose to dissolve itself rather than simply invite the African American Pentecostal leaders to join it?"

Jack Hayford responded: "We didn't want to say to our black brothers and sisters, 'Come and join our outfit.' We realize that the white person seldom recognizes the response that is required of a black person even if the invitation is accepted. Insensitivity may generate a low-grade bitterness. We didn't want to plan anything with that history, so we asked our black brothers and sisters, 'What might we do together?' And we realized that we needed to have black leadership in primary leadership at the outset" (Dupree Center for Christian Leadership, Fuller Theological Seminary, Pasadena, California).

Before we can answer who should do the changing, I am cautioned by my own experience to be careful about prejudging the motives of those who seek the joining in the first place. We all hold a fair share of blame for prejudging one another's motives, and while playing the blame game, we sometimes presume the guilt or innocence of one person or group based on the group that we are a member of. This tendency to prejudge becomes important as very different cultures seek to find common ground while carrying their ugly, well-traveled baggage of paranoia and presumption.

Numerous individuals and several mainline denominations have worked quite successfully with such dilemmas and could serve as models of how to responsibly share wealth, information, and facilities with not only inner-city, less well-off churches but also with other denominations or independent churches that are relatively small but do an effective work in the community. One shining example of this type of interracial and interdenominational support is found in the Presbyterian Church. For years, the Presbyterian Church has given money to small urban churches and shared staff and facilities with them. Its history and longevity notwithstanding, the Presbyterian Church has simply shared its resources to improve and empower smaller churches that are not Presbyterian — no fanfare, no horn tooting, and no drama about Christian unity.

Here's one concrete example of what I'm talking about: In the late 1990s, a small group from Abundant Life Christian Fellowship (membership less than two hundred), a black church in East Palo Alto, began to pray once a week with the larger Menlo Park Presbyterian Church (MPPC), a white fellowship. Abundant Life was led by senior pastor Paul Sheppard, and Menlo Pak was led by senior pastor Walt Gerber.

Seeing the vision and noting the effectiveness of the smaller church, MPPC gave a significant financial gift to Abundant Life Christian Fellowship that enabled it to acquire a worship facility.

Today Abundant Life Christian Fellowship has more than four thousand members and is one of the fastest-growing churches on the West Coast. It boasts a virtual rainbow of colors, cultures, races, and nationalities. In fact, its racial mix is so varied, it can no longer be called a "black church." At the same time, Menlo Park Presbyterian Church experienced exponential growth and today has expanded from 2,000 to well over 5,500 members on two additional campuses in San Mateo and Mountain View, California.

I have had the privilege of knowing Paul Sheppard since his preteen years. I have watched him evolve from being a "black preacher" into being a "people's preacher." I have listened to him lecture on church growth and racial reconciliation. I have heard him tell black audiences, in effect, to get over themselves, stop fighting city hall, and get on with their biblical mandate to win the lost of all colors and at any cost.

For sure, all joinings are not equal and do not happen the same way, nor do they always experience such ideal results. There are potholes and pitfalls that expose our prejudices and our presumptive natures as we seek solution to institutional religious and cultural separation. Let's look at a few.

Prejudiced Presumptions

Whenever we see a gathering of an all-black audience or organization, should we conclude that it is racist or walking in disunity; or should we assume it probably comes from an ethnically specific community? Similarly, whenever there is an all-white congregation or a predominantly white organization, should we conclude that it is racist, separatist, or walking in disunity; or should we assume it comes from a predominantly white community? In situations like these, do we leap to the conclusion that ethnic-specific communities are exclusive, meaning others need not apply? Obviously, there are many reasons for a community to be ethnically homogeneous. The question is, has the homogeneous nature of the group turned it into an ethnically exclusive group that rejects brothers and sisters who are not of their fold or, more specifically, do not look like them?

When Jackie and I moved to San Antonio's northwestern side, we did not deliberately select an all-white community in which to live. We selected our house without thought of who our neighbors would be. To our delight, the neighbors on each side of us at different times knocked on our door, introduced themselves, welcomed us to the neighborhood, gave us homemade cookies and gifts, and confessed that they were praying for "good people" to live in the house and thought their prayers had been answered.

Immediately we knew they were prejudiced; how else would they know that we were good people? How dare they label us without knowing us! Of course, I jest. While delighted with our neighbors' remarks, we were not really surprised. When we reflect on the communities we have lived in—some all-black, some all-white, and some multiracial, we conclude that we have never had a bad housing experience related to race.

We are not so naïve as to think racism has been wiped out because of our positive housing experiences. We can tell you horror stories about the fight that some black parents have faced in getting equal and excellent education and recognition for their children in predominantly white settings. Bu the point is, I have learned not to prejudge a situation before experiencing it, and I have learned not to make assumptions based on history and fear.

I have also learned that even in truly racist circumstances, my anger can prejudice and preempt the solution. I have learned instead to interject my hope, to confront and engage the problem while believing it can change. After all, reconciliation is what we Christians do. As a Christian, I choose to be a thermostat, one who determines the temperature in the room—not a thermometer, one who reflects the temperature in the room.

Is it not the *exclusion* of others, by either commission or omission, that judges us as racist, separatist, and unreconciled? In the world, we must fight racism with civil law and the supernatural advantage of faith. In the church, we must fight racism by remaining unconditionally dedicated to reconciliation and that same supernatural power that overcomes evil. If we refuse to be joined to other Christians on the basis of racial advantage, privilege, or preference, we are not discerning the body and thus bring judgment on ourselves and those we influence. Such lack of discernment comes with grave consequences. If we reject our eyes, we are blind; if we exclude our feet, we become crippled; and if we reject our hands, we render ourselves helpless and foolish.

It is the premeditated practice of exclusion that is racist. It is the intentional ignoring of the blood of Jesus that makes us all one that declares us guilty of not discerning the body. The apostle Paul said it this way:

"For we were all baptized by one Spirit into one body — whether Jews or Greeks, slave or free — and we were all given

the one Spirit to drink. Now the body is not made up of one part but of many. If the foot should say, 'Because I am not a hand, I do not belong to the body,' it would not for that reason cease to be part of the body. . . . If the whole body were an eye, where would the sense of hearing be?" (1 Cor. 12:13–15,17).

In instances where whites have abandoned the inner city, should we expect the leaders and the organizations that spring up in the inner city to be white, or should we expect the police force, the firefighters, the mayor, the political parties, the PTA, and other organizations to reflect the citizenry of the inner city? Should we live in different communities but join together to govern those communities in the name of unity? Should we have organizations that govern where they do not dwell? More specifically, should a white committee that does not dwell in the community judge a conflict, ordain a minister, or otherwise govern a black church? Is it a cover for our failure when we propose unity at the top while practicing division at the bottom?

When we are separated for reasons of cultural comfort, economic advantage, cultural traditions, or the coincidental attrition that results through relocation or other circumstances beyond our control, we can still be united by faith in one God and His one Word. It is no different from distant brothers and sisters who do whatever it takes to visit, share, and support one another.

It is neither necessary nor realistic to expect them to sell their houses and move in together, unless circumstances demand such drastic action. No conclusions need be drawn regarding racism unless one race intentionally excludes the other for reasons of race.

The unity of relatives, physical or spiritual, is best demonstrated through their cooperation and mutual support of one another regardless of distance or circumstances. In other words, unity and racial reconciliation are so much more than a disingenuous photo op or a temporary arrangement for the sake of maintaining or expanding power. The determination of who leads should always be based on who dwells; that is, the leaders of any community should come from those who actually live in the community. The institution, whether the police department or a denomination's credentialing board, should be constituted of the indigenous population.

In any case, the solution is not to dissolve the natural family and join another for the sake of appearance. We are united only when we "dwell together," as we have already noted from Psalm 133. According to the psalmist, we experience blessings and eternal life when we dwell in unity. If dwelling in unity is God's promised place of blessing and life forevermore, then perhaps the solution to the problem of racism is to fight anything that segregates or separates family members from operating and cooperating. If eternal life and blessing are to come to the inner city, then perhaps believers of all races should flood the inner city and make their dwellings there. Now that's a radical response, I know, but could this be the ultimate strategy for evangelizing our world — intentionally creating multiracial Christian ghettos? Could this be the ultimate fulfillment of the Great Commission?

Obviously, if we are not in unity with the whole body, we are missing some of our abilities and robbing the body of its full potential. It is clear to me that unity is not an option — it is a mandate. Furthermore, it is crystal clear that the biblical mandate for unity trumps exclusive memberships based on anything other than the blood of Jesus. In other words, I cannot be a member of anything that excludes a believing brother or sister. More specifically, being a Christian trumps being black, white, brown, yellow, red, or any combination thereof. The Christian community is beautified by racial diversity and distinguished by its racial unity. It is indeed a little bit of heaven on earth.

Discussion Guide

1. How can the church demonstrate unity in a de facto segregated community where the church is one race because the community is one race?

2. What are some of the ways we overreact to the biblical call to unity?

3. How can the church defeat exclusion as an attitude and hindrance to unity?

4. Should we govern where we do not dwell? When does this happen, and what are the results?

God of our Weary Years • *Dr. M. Tyrone Cushman*

Chapter 16

KINGDOM TIME

I believe the twenty-first century has ushered in the kingdom age. By *kingdom age,* I mean a period of time in which we will see increased and effective church presence and influence. The winning of souls and the changing of spiritual and moral direction, coupled with believers walking in obedience to the Word of God, fulfill the words of Matthew 6:10: "Thy kingdom come."

The arrival of the kingdom age is also evidenced by the violent pushback from the media and government in the United States and around the world. Christian values are under attack in many places, evangelism in Iraq and China meets with persecution, and Third World Islamic countries react to the advancement of the Christian gospel. This violent pushback is the fulfillment of Matthew 11:12: "From the days of John the Baptist until now, the kingdom of heaven has been forcefully advancing, and forceful men lay hold of it."

As it relates to church polity, this kingdom age will herald the restoration of apostolic authority and a dramatic decline in rule by committee or consensus church governments. The *evening church* (the church that exists just before and at the return of Jesus Christ) will begin operating in mighty demonstrations of the Spirit and power. It will be much as the apostle Paul said when writing to the Corinthian saints: "And my speech and my preaching was not with enticing words of man's wisdom, but in demonstration of the Spirit and of power: That your faith should not stand in the wisdom of men, but in the power of God" (1 Cor. 2:4–5 KJV).

Jesus confounded the religious extremists of His day by refusing to go through the usual religious channels or seek the approval of institutional leaders. He refused to use political leverage and influence. He ignored most of the protocols of His time and announced an entirely new power paradigm that so angered and threatened the religious establishment that they plotted day and night to capture and kill Him.

Jesus said, "The prince of this world cometh, and hath nothing in me" (John 14:30 KJV). Absolutely no one could take credit for Him or from Him. When some attempted to discredit Him by calling him a madman, the people spoke on His behalf, saying, "These are not the words of a man possessed by a demon. Can a demon open the eyes of the blind?" [Jn. 10:21]

Jesus was not a madman, but He operated from a different world and with a different power. The *morning church* (the early days of the New Testament church launched in the book of Acts) was launched by the same power Jesus used, a power never before witnessed in the world — the power of the Holy Spirit.

My prayer is, "Lord, may we be madmen and madwomen with a reputation for opening blinded eyes." Jesus sought only to please the Father. May we recapture Jesus' legacy of the single-mindedness that united Him with His Father and His purpose.

Ironically, the Great Commission is a command to go and make disciples of *all* nations. It may very well be that our failure to follow this command is more like the biblical story of the prophet Jonah than we care to admit. Instead of sailing to Nineveh to carry a message of warning to the Ninevites as God had ordered him to do, Jonah sailed in the opposite direction and almost caused the innocent men on his getaway boat to die in a supernatural storm. After being swallowed by a big fish, he changed his mind and obeyed God. His obedience led to the salvation of the Ninevites because they heeded his warning, repented of their sin, and avoided God's judgment (see Jonah 1–3).

Could it be that a disobedient church is the problem and that as soon as it obeys the command to go make disciples, healing and deliverance will break out in the world? Is God waiting for the church to act out His will on the earth as it is being done in heaven? Is there a divine power waiting to enable the kingdom to come on earth as it is in heaven? Could it be that we are hung up on race because we are not hung up on souls? Could it be that making disciples instead of debating doctrines and dividing into denominations over methods of baptizing is the solution in every Christian denomination?

What do you think would happen if we all just flat out went after souls? Isaiah asked, "Who has heard of such a thing? Shall the earth be made to bring forth in one day? Or shall a nation be born at once? For as soon as Zion travailed, she brought forth her children" (Isa. 66:8 KJV). This prophecy regarding Zion, or the church, was fulfilled on the day of Pentecost. In the upper room, the followers of the ascended Christ gathered and travailed in prayer like a woman in labor. As a result, the Holy Spirit was poured out, and three thousand souls were born in one day. This was a simultaneous birthing, empowering, and launching of the kingdom of God, which is the New Testament church. Thy kingdom come; Thy will be done!

The promised Holy Ghost came upon them that day, and they witnessed with new boldness and new power. The promise of Jesus began to be fulfilled in the New Testament church:

And these signs will accompany those who believe; in my name they will drive out demons, they will speak in new tongues; they will pick up snakes with their hands; and when they drink deadly poison, it will not hurt them at all; they will place their hands on sick people, and they will get well. After the Lord Jesus had spoken to them, he was taken up into heaven and he sat at the right hand of God. Then the disciples went out and preached everywhere, and the Lord worked with them and confirmed his word by the signs that accompanied it.

—Mark 16:17–29

The legacy of the evening-light church will be Zechariah's prophecy: "But it shall come to pass, that at evening time it shall be light" (Zech.14:7). Now is the most exciting time in history. It is also the most challenging. Prophets and prophecies, both real and imagined, are everywhere. False doctrines descend like an evening fog, causing confusion and conflict among the faithful. But the anecdote for false doctrine, false prophets, false religions, false hope, and spirits of division, racism, and bigotry is found in two simple kingdom strategies: unconditional love and the ministry of reconciliation.

We must consume ourselves with these kingdom messages. I am thoroughly convinced that these biblical strategies will fulfill the Master's prayer, "Thine is the kingdom and the power and the glory forever and ever, amen."

Discussion Guide

1. What contemporary events identify the kingdom age?

2. How do racial, gender, class, and economic reconciliation fit into a kingdom-of-God strategy?

3. What should be the top three priorities in the kingdom of God?

4. What is the message of the kingdom?

Chapter 17

THE DANGER OF ORTHODOXY

The complexities of canonization and beatification notwithstanding, Vivian Beatrice Cushman, my mother, was a "Saint." Yes, that's exactly what I mean: a capital *S* saint. She was voted into sainthood by her seven children. It was unanimous. I feel sure that if the pope were to eat some of her peach cobbler and macaroni and cheese, he too would waive the Roman Catholic Church's long and formal procedures, cut to the chase, and make the declaration—Saint Vivian.

Along with her vaunted culinary skills, my mother was the most patient, kind, and praying woman I have ever known. Her wisdom was recognized and celebrated throughout the Eight Mile Road housing project and then up and down Anglin street in Detroit, Michigan, where we lived. People from all walks of life came to our house, seeking my mother's advice and the laying on of her loving hands in prayer for healing and deliverance from all kinds of bondage.

One bright summer day, when I was eleven years old, I burst into the kitchen as she was preparing dinner in order to ask her some serious questions, questions so serious they kept me awake at night. "Mama, if a baby dies before it's old enough to hear about Jesus, will it go to heaven?" I asked. Before she could answer, I asked my follow-up question: "And will the people in the darkest part of Africa who have never heard of Jesus be lost and go to hell?"

She gave me her classic first response: "What do you think?"

"Well, I don't think it would be fair if people who didn't ask to be born in the first place and then didn't hear about Jesus and don't know any better would go to hell. And I think God is fair," I added.

She looked at me with hope in her gaze. Her voice lowered, as if to say, "This is off the record." Then she answered, "Well, I also think He's fair; and even more than being fair, I think He is so wise and loving that He has figured that out already. That's why He needs you to grow up and carry the gospel as far and wide as you can. I am sure He will do the rest."

I remember walking away thinking, *But that's not what they said in Sunday school.*

Thanks to those simple words from Saint Vivian, and in spite of Sunday school, Bible college, university, forty-plus years as a pastor, and five years as general overseer of my denomination, my mother's wisdom has outlasted the rigid orthodoxies of my Holiness tradition. As I travel around the world, I am fascinated by the many wonderful manifestations of goodwill and genuine human kindness practiced by believers of many different denominational stripes who love God with all their heart, mind, body, and soul.

As a young man, I was always depressed by the thought that so many were going to spend eternity in hell unless I could reach them with the gospel of Jesus Christ . . . and lead them into receiving baptism by submersion in water . . . and then the baptism in the Holy Ghost . . . then persuade them to attend a church called by the only name in the New Testament given for a church, the "Church of God" . . . and then have them become a part of the Reformation movement of the Church of God because it was God's "last reformation" . . . and show them how to embrace this nondenominational church's emphasis on unity (even though it sometimes practiced racial division) . . . walk in holiness of lifestyle . . . and practice the gifts of the Spirit — well at least some of the gifts, even though some of us practiced all of them . . . etc., etc., etc. I think you get the picture.

Deep inside I knew God had not left the world He died for in the hands of well-meaning though often confused Christian believers, so I did what most who have been on this Christian journey for any appreciable length of time eventually do. First, I moderated my view of how I understood the Word of God. Second, I accepted that God was bigger than my church background (after all, the Church of God was only two hundred thousand strong). Third, I concluded that the truth was not relative but context was and that God was more generous, accepting, and inclusive than I had been taught. It occurred to me if we (the Church of God) were all God had, God was in trouble!

I still believe that God came down from heaven to earth in the form of Jesus; that He died on the cross for my sins; that He rose from the dead and ascended into heaven; that He came back as promised in the form of the Holy Ghost (okay, "Holy Spirit") for the purpose of enabling us to have power over sin, the evil one, and self; and that He gave us power to establish His kingdom in the earth. But I also believe the way that is walked out by each of us is determined only by God Himself, who factors in variables of context; opportunity; background; and the breadth and depth of His love, grace, and mercy. I describe this as "a generous orthodoxy," to borrow the term used in the title of Brian D. McLaren's book by the same name.

The late Dr. Horace W. Sheppard Sr., the greatest preacher I have ever heard, was famous for declaring himself "Catholic, because I believe the church is the universal body of Christ; Baptist, because I have been to the water; Church of God, because I believe the church belongs to God; Methodist, because I methodically study and try to adopt His method; Pentecostal, because I have been baptized in the Holy Ghost like on the day of Pentecost; Jehovah's Witness, because Jehovah is His name and I am one of His witnesses." Of course, by the time he finished, he had covered every denomination he could think of, and the members of the audience were on their feet, shouting back with great joy and affirmation, regardless of whether they really agreed with him.

There is great danger in orthodoxy, not because of any one doctrinal or theological emphasis, but because of the potential and practice of exclusion that stems from it. The Greek word *orthodoxos,* from which we get the English word *orthodoxy,* literally means "of the right opinion." But who determines that right opinion? That spirit of exclusion and division that orthodoxy can easily though unintentionally promote has been spiritual kryptonite to the body of Christ throughout the ages.

The developing of common-sense Christian faith in this high-tech, postmodern, ecumenical, relativistic, and humanistic age is neither simple nor certain and probably requires some supernatural intervention. It is clear to me that our extremes evolve from sacred opinions that crystallize and solemnize into orthodoxies that are then rehearsed for the ages. These orthodoxies take on a history and life of their own, fixed doctrines developed from fixed theologies that, over time, become the standard beliefs that form religious foundation and define the purist sect within any religious body. They are the "orthodox" believers, believers who tolerate little variance and no compromise, no matter what the evolution of revelatory truth should bring.

Brian D. McLaren, in his book *A Generous Orthodoxy,* writes:

Some defend this time-honored approach, saying that the Holy Spirit always protects the true church from making mistakes, so all those whom the true church (i.e., theirs) judges unorthodox truly are. This book . . . agrees that where the Holy Spirit is shown the door by the church, an unlocked window is found through which the Spirit will sneakily enter. Thus the Holy Spirit stubbornly refuses to abandon the church even when the church quenches the Spirit— all in spite of the fact that the church has little idea how unorthodox it is at any given moment. While this view is humbling for the church, it also holds out the hope that if a church can't yet be perfectly orthodox, it can—with the Holy Spirit's help and by the grace of God—at least be perpetually reformable. (p. 35)

It is the tightly held orthodoxies that more often than not perpetuate toxic understandings and lead to deadly intolerance and damaging extremes that really do more harm than good. It is equally clear to me that religious orthodoxy has inadvertently aided and abetted the social crimes of racism, sexism, denominationalism, and classism. Furthermore, these acts against humanity have enjoyed the cover of strong and enduring theological tradition defined as orthodoxy. Sexism, for example, is illustrated in the ancient Jewish doctrines of divorce and remarriage that made the putting away of a woman a male privilege. Over time, this law was abused to the extent that women could be put away for any cause. But when Jesus stepped onto the scene, He declared that "in the beginning it was not so" (Matt. 19:8).

The orthodox Pharisees who challenged Jesus for healing on the Sabbath had to be reminded by Jesus that man was not made for the Sabbath, but the Sabbath was made for man. Modern-day Pharisees in many Christian churches, because of unbending and unreasonable conservative views against divorce, still cling to beliefs and traditions that hold women in marriages where they are brutalized. To this day, Christians who hold to an extreme conservative orthodoxy sometimes justify the enslavement of blacks in particular by erroneously citing the so-called curse of Ham in Genesis 9:24 or the endorsement of the institution of slavery in general from an erroneous and self-serving interpretation of the apostle Paul's exhortation to slaves in Ephesians 6:5, 9.

The point is, the error of interpretation has historically shaped our orthodoxies and sanctified toxic and socially damaging theologies, creating the irony of complicity and the spectacle of theological contradiction. As a result, we have churches that are purposely all white because of their belief that mixing the races is against Scripture; and we have others that are all black because they have erroneously chosen to pursue racial justice as a precondition for biblical reconciliation and continue to grind the proverbial axe.

Jesus' birth heralded a new beginning for all peoples. He launched a new paradigm relative to race, gender, and nationality. He broke with the strict orthodoxy of His Jewish faith and cut across the expectation of faithless non-Jews. He disregarded religious protocols and set loose a nuclear chain reaction that launched the all-inclusive kingdom of God. His coming fulfilled God's covenant promise to Abraham when He said, "All the people of the earth will be blessed through you" (Gen.12:3).

This fulfillment began with the prophetic declaration from Simeon in Luke 2:30–32: "For my eyes have seen your salvation, which you have prepared in the sight of all people, a light for revelation to the Gentiles and for the glory to your people Israel." It culminated with great clarity when the apostle Peter confronted his racist orthodoxy in a vision and was told, "Do not call anything impure that God has made clean" (Acts 10:15).

Following Peter's personal revelation, we see an even more powerful public revelation: "He [Peter] said to them: 'You are well aware that it is against our law for a Jew to associate with a Gentile or visit him. . . . Then Peter began to speak: 'I now realize how true it is that God does not show favoritism' " (Acts 10:28, 34). This revelation united the Old and New Testament churches and established the new covenant precedent of multiracial and multinational unity in the kingdom of God.

Religious orthodoxy began dying a slow death that day, and the process continues. Indeed, in today's church, we fight the revival of religious orthodoxy with the same two spiritual weapons used in the early church: the Word, as seen in Peter speaking God's Word to the house of Cornelius; and the Spirit: "While Peter was still speaking these words, the Holy Spirit came on all who heard the message" (Acts 10:44). God's Word and God's Spirit compose the two-edged sword of spiritual warfare. The Word and the Spirit are the silver bullets designed to kill the spirit of division and its ugly offspring — racism and denominationalism.

Discussion Guide

1. Is it possible for us to know all there is to know or all that is necessary to know? What does that say about what you know now?

2. Describe the difference between religious orthodoxy and Bible truth.

3. How does religious orthodoxy influence your Christian faith?

4. Describe Jesus' contempt for religious orthodoxy. Identify your church or denomination's orthodoxies.

Chapter 18

THE CHURCH'S DIRTY LITTLE SECRET:
From Reformation to Revolution

Historical ecclesiology includes the church's dirty little secret of racial division. In fact, it can be argued that the church did as much or more to perpetuate and institutionalize slavery as any other organization in the world. Perhaps this is the reason I am so convinced it will take the restored church to break the bondage of racism.

The church has been in bed with the secular world from the days of the emperor Constantine, who mandated that Christianity become the official state religion and launched the imperialization of Christianity. In so doing, he corrupted the church's chief principle of salvation by faith alone.

This trend continued from the fourth century forward, as seen in the doctrine commonly referred to as "divine right." This doctrine in defense of monarchical absolutism asserted that kings derived their authority from God and could not, therefore, be held accountable for their actions by any earthly authority, such as a parliament. Originating in Europe, the divine-right theory can be traced to the medieval conception of God's award of temporal power to the political ruler, paralleling the award of spiritual favor and authority (Richard Hooker, *The European Enlightenment Glossary: The Divine Right of Kings,* 1999).

This self-serving doctrine corrupted imperial Christianity and put the "blue" in the blood of so-called royalty. The effect was to perpetuate and even make sacred the notion of divine dynasties, bloodlines, and class distinctions. The most devastating of satanic strategies was sprung as the Christian church, under the cover and protection of the state, supported slavery, classism, and eventually racism.

The phenomenon of racism in the church is historical and perhaps explains its deep entrenchment in our spiritual as well as our social psyches, especially as it relates to the dominant culture. For example, until recently the Mormons' rejection of black elders mocked their claims of openness and brought wide and unwanted scrutiny and criticism from a skeptical public media. The Roman Catholic Church's failure to speak out against Hitler's slaughter of the Jews continues to haunt their religious legacy to this day. In the United States in particular, some in the evangelical Christian movement, which is populated by many mainline denominations, argues for the separation of the races based on the errant belief that blacks, as descendants of Noah's son Ham, are cursed to be the servants of others.

Consequently, divisions of all kinds, but especially racism, mock our claim that God is not a respecter of persons and spoil our feast of charity. Like a dormant virus that triggers periodic eruptions, it corrupts entire denominations and defies moves of God dedicated to racism's destruction.

I want to share both a history that will lend perspective and a synoptical but real-world case history that illustrates how racism has threaded its way through religion and embedded itself in society with a silent nod of tolerance, if not approval, from the institution sent to destroy it—the church. I will relate the case history of two movements that struggle to define and live out the very core value they were founded upon. These two organizations are not alone in their dilemma; though small, they are symbolic of a spiritual warfare being waged within denominations and reformation movements all over the world. Those who are fighting through to victory in spite of their histories and pride, however, are experiencing tremendous triumphs and taking great territories for the kingdom of God.

A History

In the sixteenth century, salvation by faith in Jesus Christ alone lit up a bleary religious sky, gave new hope to countless generations, and marked a return to the simplicity of the gospel of the kingdom: "that God was reconciling the world to himself in Christ, not counting men's sins against them" (2 Cor. 5:19). Martin Luther must have shuddered and quaked in his frail body as he wrestled with the enormous implications of this simple message. The apostasy of his beloved church could no longer share space in a heart illumined by divine revelation. "The just shall live by faith" were words that invaded his dreams and broke into his reality, urging him to speak and forbidding him to keep silent.

That night, he rose from his knees as a prophet fresh from the presence of the same God who told Elijah to challenge the status quo and face off with the wicked wit of "that woman Jezebel" by confronting her prophets. That night, with a willing spirit and wilting flesh, Martin Luther picked up his notes recorded while listening to the voice of God and headed for the Wittenberg cathedral.

As revolutionary as his gospel was, as prophetic and powerful as his ministry came to be, Martin Luther was consumed with the now. There was no tomorrow. He was convinced that it would all end here and now. He was sure that this was the ultimate correction. On October 31, 1517, Martin Luther nailed his Ninety-five Theses on the door of the Wittenberg cathedral, and the Protestant revolution was on. The restoration of the New Testament church was underway.

Martin Luther did not see nor did he prophesy the next reformation, which would be led by John and Charles Wesley in the year 1723. John Wesley expressly requested that the movement called the Holy Club not be named after him. A sovereign move of God again ignited revival fires to renew, restore, and reconcile the church with His most prominent characteristic: His holiness. Holiness as a way of life began to spread around the world. However, established mainline denominations fought its rise in the name of God, believing this encroachment was from the kingdom of darkness.

John Wesley's movement unintentionally became the Methodist Church. It soon gave way to another move of God called the Great Awakening. Ignited by Jonathan Edwards, an American preacher and theologian, the Great Awakening became the greatest revival of the gospel of the kingdom the world had ever seen. Like a wild field fire, it swept the country and leaped the oceans to nations near and far. It spread to the four corners of the earth, but it was not the last revival or reformation.

Daniel Sidney Warner heard the beat of a far-off and different drummer pounding out yet another message of reformation, restoration, and reconciliation. "In 1878 D. S. Warner wrote: 'The Lord . . . gave me a new commission to join holiness and all truth together and build up the apostolic church of the living God.' Brother Warner and his associates, discerning the impossibility of the true church existing within the framework of denominationalism, declared their freedom from the 'sin of sectism and division' and instituted the evening light restoration movement in the latter part of the 19th century" (*Birth of a Reformation*, p. 5).

For his message to be heard, D. S. Warner soon discovered he had to leave the organization to which he had been born, realizing he could not reform it from within. He could not overcome the volume of more respected voices and soon learned the crippling power of institutionalized religion. As an insider, he could not compete with commissioned, credentialed, and experienced operatives dedicated to the preservation of the institution and its sacred history.

From within, he appeared to himself and to the angry gatekeepers of his denomination, not as a prophet with revelation, but as a radical sowing division. He was the not-so-favorite-son full of words that seemed to disrespect and deny both the history and the heritage of the Winebrenarians, the faith of his fathers.

In 1880, led by D. S. Warner, the Church of God Reformation movement was born with all the great power, purpose, and excitement of a new move of God. This movement spread far and gloriously fast as its message of unity grew out of its dedication to destroy sectarianism and denominationalism. Soon, however, the leaders and the young movement experienced the resistance, taunts, and threats experienced by all reformers and reform movements. Racism raised its ugly head. The young movement was challenged to move through the social evils it had been birthed to reform and to change or succumb to the pressure to accommodate its own need for peace, respect, acceptance, and the continued support of fellow reformation pioneers.

The choice was painfully clear and shamefully familiar. Would the new movement become an institution dedicated to its own end: the protection of the purity of its reform ideology; or would it press forward with a broader call: to reform the secular and social evils surrounding it? Would it become fishers of all men or keepers of the aquarium? Would it be the kingdom of God or just another religious reformation?

Events were fluid. Spiritual revelation came face-to-face with real-world conditions. The surge of events urged them to redefine their vision to become intentionally inclusive or to go with the socially accepted racial segregation of their time.

Success had forced them into enemy territory: what to do about the Negroes who were hearing and believing the call to come out of religious Babylon and denominationalism in favor of Christ, holiness, and unity. It quickly became apparent that the come-outers were being called out.

The Church of God Reformation movement seemed to move faster than its revelation as it pondered the issue of mixing with other races. In retrospect, the infant movement was more immature than it was racist. In fact, I have come to believe that with a few exceptions, they were not racist at all. They were victims of an inherited curse. They were sure that the revelation that launched them came to break down denominational walls, but when trouble came, they were not so sure their revelation of reformation included the breaking down of racial walls.

One of their most glorious hymns was not enough to stem the tide of reformational retreat, even as they sang:

> Christians all should join together in the bonds of peace;
> All the clashing of opinions, all the strife should cease.
> Let divisions be forsaken and the holy join in one
> And the will of God in all be done.

> Chorus:

> Oh, the reformation glory;
> Let it shine through every land.
> We will tell the gospel story,
> And in its truth we e'er shall stand.

> [The Reformation Glory; A. L. Byers-C. W. Naylor;
> Evening Light Songs; 1923; pg.10]

Emboldened by the perceived indecision, the agents of evil and darkness moved swiftly to exploit the human fears of a young reformation movement born in the middle of Satan's stronghold. The Ku Klux Klan terrorized their tent revivals with whips, guns, and horses, beating the worshipers, setting fire to tents, and threatening their lives, should they continue their "nigger-lovin' religion" and their race mixing.

Here's an account from one source of what those proponents of unity faced:

The work among the colored people throughout the South was opened up by both white and Negro preachers. . . . Late in the nineteenth century (1897) the Alabama state camp meeting, held some miles out from Hartselle, was attended by both races, with only a rope stretched down the middle of the tent as a recognition of segregation. . . . One day Lena Shoffner preached a sermon about tearing down the middle wall of partition. Someone took the rope down and whites and blacks knelt at the same altar together. That night a mob came in wild fury. They threw dynamite under the boardinghouse and the camp houses and ferreted out the preachers like hounds hunting rabbits. The preachers fled. One man stood in a creek all night. Another preacher put on a woman's clothes and escaped. (C. E. Brown, D.D., *When The Trumpet Sounded,* Warner Press, p. 266)

Accounts more violent than these chronicled the early years of a noble reformation movement that lit not only the fires of religious reformation but also social revolution.

In the background, a unique music seemed to partner and patronize this new movement. Words and melodies fashioned by men and women drunk with this new wine and driven by the new wind of reformation began to define the doctrines and spell out the hopes and beliefs of a new breed of Christians — the come-outers.

The music of the Church of God Reformation movement was almost as important as its message. They continued to sing of their hope even as they began to make the critical decisions that would defy their purpose and marginalize their effectiveness:

God sets his members each in place according to His will;
Apostles, prophets, teachers, all His purpose to fulfill.

Chorus:

Oh, Church of God, I love thy courts;
Thou mother of the free;
Thou blessed home of all the saved;
I dwell content in thee.

[O Church Of God; C. W. Naylor-A. L. Byers;
Hymnal of The Church Of God; 1922; pg.413]

This verse and others soon mocked the church's divine call, and it was soon marked for decline as Negroes began to invade their powerful revivals and camp meetings in search of the unity of purpose and fellowship that was the message of the movement.

In approximately 1881 (some say as late as 1886), a black woman by the name of Jane Williams heard the voice of God and began to preach a message of sanctification and holiness foreign to the mainline denominations around her. It was the same revelation of holiness revealed to John Wesley. It was the same revelation of unity and holiness revealed to D. S. Warner.

Introduced to the Church of God by a *Gospel Trumpet* magazine found in a bus station, Jane Williams became a reformer herself, teaching and preaching under powerful and divine favor and causing no small stir in the towns and villages of South Carolina. She soon made contact with the white Anderson brethren, and in a unique partnership, they planted Church of

God congregations in South Carolina and Georgia that spread throughout the South.

Almost simultaneously (within the same decade), another band of believers disenchanted with denominational contradictions began a prayer meeting in the home of one in their group. They became known by their doctrinal emphasis and were called the Brothers and Sisters of Love.

The Tale of Two Cities

The story that follows links the Church of God Reformation movement with the National Association of the Church of God in a tortured twist of culture, history, truth, and tradition. This story is one of many case histories that demonstrate the sovereign move of God in reformation, restoration, and reconciliation of the body of Christ. It raises and answers questions about race that have national implications. It is a living example of how deep is the divide and enduring the conditioning that is the legacy of racism.

This ongoing true story suggests the dynamic nature of truth. It confirms God as the only righteous judge and leaves us to understand that no generation, denomination, or reformation owns the truth of the kingdom. When God moves in our time, it is never His last—only His latest.

History is extremely important. It is a rearview mirror that teaches us heritage as we drive prophetically forward to our destinies. History gives any people perspective and becomes a benchmark by which to measure both progress and regress. When we as a minority allow others to tell our history, it inevitably affects the self-esteem of the generations that follow, lowering ceilings, setting boundaries, and limiting promise. When we tell our own story, however, we protect our children from defaming half-truths and blatant lies. We set the record straight, even if it is for no one but ourselves.

In 1886, the Brothers and Sisters of Love of Sharon, Pennsylvania, celebrated the same revelation as did D. S. Warner and Jane Williams. Inspired by a member's dream, they purchased over a hundred acres of land in the beautiful rolling hills of West Middlesex, Pennsylvania. The fledgling group began to grow in leaps and bounds. They were African American believers who, fleeing the brutal lynchings and racism of the South, sought freedom, fellowship, and opportunity in the less volatile North. In 1916, they formed what we know today as the National Association of the Church of God.

In only a short time, the two movements, the Church of God Reformation movement and the National Association of the Church of God, formed a cooperative link under the banner of the Reformation Movement of the Church of God. Tragically, in the early 1920s, at a meeting in Augusta, Georgia, that old nemesis, racism, reared its ugly head to mock the signature doctrine of unity. At the suggestion of white leaders pressured by the violence perpetrated by the Ku Klux Klan, blacks were encouraged to evangelize blacks and whites to evangelize whites. As a result, a thriving reformation movement became a monument, and instantly the spirit and light of their original purpose, the priesthood and unity of all believers, began to fade.

From that year to this very day, while its institutions have grown ever more sophisticated with ministries stretching around the world, the Church of God Reformation movement continues to search for its soul. Its voice was lost in its formative immaturity, which led to an attempt to accommodate its fear of a racist mob and the fear of a few church leaders who felt too many blacks were coming to the campground. Thankfully, as in every reformational transition (such as the Assemblies of God and their split with the Church of God in Christ), a remnant survived to tell the story of fighting through the tension of truth and tradition to continue the work of keeping the unity of the faith in the bond of peace.

More than eighty years later, the Church of God (Anderson, Indiana) has fought to maintain the image of its hope and purpose. In the sixties, the issues of race and racism exploded again. Under the dark clouds of urban unrest, with its riots, burnings, and widespread civil unrest, whites abandoned the inner cities in droves and took their churches with them. When the dust of this massive exodus settled, major urban areas were dominated by blacks, and the surrounding suburbs became white enclaves.

A few years ago, I wrote to my dear friend and partner Wayne Harting, who pastored one of the rare white inner-city churches. Together we worked hard to bring about racial unity among the Churches of God in Detroit, Michigan. The following is a few lines from that letter:

> My, it has been a long time since the days in Detroit when we held such hope for unity and lofty dreams of cooperative ventures between the churches. To look at Detroit now, one would never know we attended such meetings or ever worked on such lofty dreams, since there are no white Churches of God in the city of Detroit.
>
> Our *practice* of the doctrine of unity never materialized beyond a few good-feeling gatherings. The actions of the fleeing churches spoke volumes about their true beliefs. Reconciliation was once again relegated to the laboratory, the Church of God movement lost another opportunity to "move," and our movement became a monument of high ideals.
>
> Northwestern Church of God, State Fair Church of God, and Eastside Church of God are all gone or are monocultural monuments to our failure to live out the true meaning of our doctrine. These were the white churches of my generation . . . gone. They did not evangelize their changing communities. They did not integrate. They moved to the relative safety and sanctity of suburbia. They did what their early Reformation ancestors

did in the South that led to the racial divide we now struggle to bridge—they accommodated their fears.

Today in the Church of God, the whites have their ministry headquarters in Anderson, Indiana, and the blacks have their headquarters in West Middlesex, Pennsylvania. Out of approximately 2,300 churches in the United States and Canada, approximately 1,800 are all white, and approximately 400 are all black. As a natural consequence, most have their separate regional assemblies, credentialing committees, conferences, conventions, and camp meetings—all of which were born out of sacred histories, cultures, and traditions.

A dwindling number of blacks attend the annual North American Convention of the Church of God held in Anderson, Indiana, while a very small token number of whites attend the annual (black) camp meeting of the National Association of the Church of God. Appearances are maintained through seasonal exchanges of goodwill gestures and public Kodak moments.

Here is the conclusion of this matter: I am sure that the hearts of our leaders in Anderson are in the right place. I believe that most continue to dream of one church, under God, indivisible. I am equally sure that key leaders in both camps are too steeped in "Reformation worship" or "Zion's Hill worship" to realize the paradigm has shifted and the train for change has left the station with the next generation aboard.

Confused about how to overcome the stigmas of past generations and determined to find a face-saving way back to the unity we preached, we are suddenly facing an ever-decreasing window of opportunity to influence the next generation. We must now repent and forgive ourselves for past racial indiscretions, disentangle ourselves from the purpose-freezing paralysis of analysis, and go before God in fasting and prayer for a new, relevant way forward. Based on the principle that the best defense is a good offense, the way forward, in my opinion, will be the adoption of a twenty-first-century comprehensive message and ministry of reconciliation.

Discussion Guide

1. What is your opinion of the churches historical role in society? What should have been the Roman Catholic position during the rise of Hitler?

2. Identify the religious patterns, revolutions and events that have given shape to the Christian church.

3. Identify a religious reformer or reformation movement of the past 50 years.

4. What do you "see" will be the role of religion in general and the Christian church in particular in society in the next 50 years?

Chapter 19

REVOLUTION, THE PRECURSOR TO REVIVAL

The Church of God in Anderson, Indiana, and in West Middlesex, Pennsylvania, will live, but only through the men and women they have trained to engage the revolution. These organizations will act as the bridge that links, launches, and liberates Generation Next.

Generation Next is the generation that knows not Emmett Till; the four little girls killed in the bombing of their church in Birmingham, Alabama; Viola Luizzo; Andrew Goodman, James Chaney, and Michael Schwerner; Medgar Evers; and other martyrs of "the Struggle." This generation is not full of maddening memories of racial injustice. They are the Barack Obama generation, with high idealistic expectations. Their religion is uncomplicated by ancient theologies, divisive doctrines, and irrelevant rituals.

Generation Next is revolutionizing the way church is done. They find bigotry curious. They do not give sanction or sanctuary to racist behavior. Wearied by their parents' strict structures and long memories, they practice a more flexible if not liberal orthodoxy that emphasizes unity of purpose and making a difference. They do not hold on to things that do not work, whether a broken marriage or a broken belief system. They seem more likely to celebrate diversity than to deliberate it.

In one of his greatest speeches, presidential contender Barack Obama eloquently and accurately explained this in his speech about attaining a more perfect union. He said, "For the men and women of *this* generation, the memories of humiliation and doubt and fear have not gone away; nor has the anger and the bitterness of those years. That anger may not get expressed in public, in front of white coworkers or white friends. But it does find voice in the barbershop or around the kitchen table."

Generation Next is more inclined to show you how they feel than to tell you. They vote with their feet and their wallets. My generation threatened revolution, but the coming generation is bringing revolution to the church and beyond.

The Restoration of the Local Congregation

I am thoroughly convinced the world will change through the message and influence of the collective local church. In fact, it was the house church that came to be defined as the body of Christ and the center of activity for new believers in the early church.

In the early church, there arose a need for a major policy decision regarding racial mixing. The leaders of the church each came from their individual cities and provinces. James, the chief apostle, had them send a directive to the local churches where the action was taking place.

The Council of Jerusalem discussed in Acts 15 was a key link in the apostolic chain of command. They did not meet because of actions initiated in the council; they met because of the very fluid events taking place in the local assemblies. These were defining moments in the early days of the developing church. The apostles' spiritual gifts equipped them with the wisdom and authority to advise the leaders of the local churches. The spirit of submission, coupled with the delegated authority of the Jerusalem apostles, gave the other key apostolic links (prophets, evangelists, pastors, and teachers) the authority necessary to carry out these apostolic directives.

In the early days of the kingdom of God, God did not operate without gifted leaders, leaders were not effective without gifted subordinate leaders, and those subordinate leaders were useless without gifted self-subordinated followers. The leaders of the early church were feeling their way. They said, "It *seemed* good to the Holy Ghost and to us . . ." (Acts 15:28, emphasis added). With intact leadership, their mission was successful, for the Bible says that when "they gathered the church together and delivered the letter . . . the people read it and were glad for its encouraging message" (Acts 15:31).

Having established order, the young church was ready to meet the challenges from within and without. They had to deal with the lingering prejudice of one of the apostles. Later they engaged the brutal policies of city government. They were forced to go before the likes of King Agrippa, handle the riots in the city of Ephesus, and intervene through intercessory prayer to break Peter out of prison. They had to teach the management of spiritual gifts in the church at Corinth, and they dealt with racial, religious, and gender discrimination in the church of Galatia.

In the first century, the local church was the exclusive representative of the kingdom of God. In the twenty-first century, I believe we will witness a return of the power and influence of the local congregation. Already we see local churches outgrowing the need to be governed or guided by permanently established denominational headquarters. Instead, without burning the bridges that link them to their histories, they have formally declared themselves as independent fellowships voluntarily affiliated with the organizations.

For example, Bishop T. D. Jakes, senior pastor of the Potter's House, which is one of the largest churches in America, is affiliated with an apostolic denomination but operates independently of denominational governance. Bishop G. A. Thompson, senior pastor of Jubilee Christian Church International, the largest church in New England, is affiliated with the Church of God (Anderson, Indiana) but operates absolutely independently from it as it relates to government.

Many larger churches are well able to send missionary expeditions directly from their congregations. They no longer send funds to a department in the denominational headquarters to do for them what they can do for themselves. Furthermore, small bodies of house churches are springing up around the country and around the world with a greater hands-on approach to community ministry that is more efficient and effective than any organizational hierarchy. Even the U.S. government has recognized the effectiveness of the local church and has begun to directly collaborate with it through federally funded faith-based initiatives that affect communities directly and more efficiently.

I sincerely believe the civil rights movement was most effective when it used the local church as its base of operation. Once it dissolved into the Southern Christian Leadership Council (SCLC), however, it lost momentum and then effectiveness. The Nobel Peace Prize–winning Dr. Martin Luther King Jr. was the twentieth-century apostle, prophet, and senior pastor of Ebenezer Baptist Church. Some would even call him the apostle Paul of our time, but his effectiveness was in direct proportion to his connection to the local churches.

When the black church in particular and subsequently the black and white church in general became involved in the outrage of racial violence against peaceful demonstrators, everything changed. Things changed because the church on earth finally lined up with the will of God in heaven, thus bringing to pass the fulfillment of Scripture: "Thy kingdom come; Thy will be done on earth as it is in heaven."

The awful spirit of division has vomited upon God's creation the racism, sexism, and classism that we have struggled with for millennia. But it can be defeated in our time if the local church will reassume its position as point man and engage this enemy with the weapons of our warfare, apostolic order and spiritual gifts, at the street level.

We must take the fight to the streets. There are more of us than there are of them, for we are surrounded by chariots of fire, battalions of supernatural warriors waiting for us to engage the real battle. The cavalry is ready but can respond only to our need and our call. A demand must be placed on the supply. Those who have discovered this simple secret are going forth conquering and doing exploits in the name of our God and King.

Great and gifted leaders like T. D. Jakes and Rick Warren, who lead two of the largest, most effective churches in the world, have risen to the challenge. They have organized the local body so well that they have planted churches, fed the hungry, clothed the naked, launched prison ministries, opened child-care centers, and sheltered the homeless far more than most denominational organizations. I truly believe it is because they operate within the prerequisite principles of the fivefold ministry of Ephesians 4:11. Many other churches great and small operate with the same success for the same reason and are taking dominion wherever they place their feet.

It is here, at the local level, that the church must face the foe and become the enemy of bigotry and racism. In the local church I attend, my pastor, Bishop Rick Hawkins, has stated uncompromisingly that we will not tolerate bigotry, prejudice, or racism of any kind from anyone. Many other churches are doing the same.

The local church is the most effective tool God has on the earth. The local churches *united* constitute the kingdom of God, and only the local churches united as the kingdom of God have the power to subdue the spirit of division and exercise dominion as the movers and shakers of their communities.

As God's prophet in Pasadena, California, for twenty-two years, I did not pastor the largest church, but I will tell you that no one was more effective in community relations than Pasadena Church of God. At the risk of sounding immodest, I must say we enjoyed the confidence of the police chief and the mayor. When trouble came to the city, we were called upon to speak a word of peace. When the mayor had an initiative he wanted to present, we were invited to share the perspective of the church. When gangs were ruling the streets, we gathered the churches across racial and denominational lines and took to the streets in a massive march led by the men of the city and their sons. The police chief Bernard Melekian, men and women of the city council marched with us. It marked the beginning of a new season of dramatic dissipation of gang activity in our city.

When three children were killed on Halloween night in 1993, our church and other churches declared war on the murderers by fasting and praying and accessing the supernatural power given to the church to defeat evil. To find and prosecute the criminals, Pasadena Church of God, Lake Avenue Congregational, New Revelation Baptist, Victory Bible, and other key congregations representing all races in the city operated behind the scenes in a world unknown to city hall. We asked God to make the criminals brag to the wrong person, talk in their sleep, or break down with guilt. In a matter of days, the murderers were found. You guessed it—one bragged to a friend, and another broke down and also identified the third.

This all happened within days of these churches' declaration of war and united dedication to warfare praying. This is the awesome power of the local churches united. As chaotic as our world is, remove the church for twenty-four hours and this earth would not be fit for human habitation.

In a simple way, I have tried to disclose, define, and describe some of the histories, both biblical and secular, that have brought us to this place. I am unashamedly suggesting that the church is the hope of the world and that the world at its worst needs the church at its best. However, the truth is, the church has been so infiltrated and influenced by the world that she has been compromised and marginalized in her effectiveness.

Nevertheless, I prophesy to you in the words of the old folks after a protracted illness, "She is coming back this way!" We have the right message, the message of reconciliation; we have the right champion, the resurrected Jesus Christ; and we are in the right place, the church, God's kingdom on earth.

The local churches are the first responders in the kingdom of God and have divine authority to exercise dominion where they are planted. It is, therefore, imperative that the local church present itself as the model of true community: inclusive, tolerant, compassionate, and trustworthy. And when there is a fight, it must engage.

We must not allow ourselves to be lobbied by special interests that promise gifts, money, and worldly influence if we keep quiet. We must not seek ill-gotten gains from secular alliances with promises of privilege, power, prestige, or position in exchange for our spiritual power and influence in city hall. The church united represents the kingdom of God exclusively. It is not for sale or for hire.

Racism and all its cousins is a viral curse, and God's church is the anecdote. We must kill this virus without compromise. We already know that if we do not kill the virus, it will first compromise and then kill us.

Discussion Guide

1. Define Generation Next.

2. What role did apostolic leadership play in the early church?

3. Wherein lies the effectiveness of the local church?

4. Identify successful local churches. What pattern can we see in them? What do they have in common?

Chapter 20

THE PRESCRIPTION

I want to suggest three characteristics that must exist before there can be serious across-the-board reconciliation, whether between races, churches, family members, or friends. I encourage you to customize this discussion to your unique community and use it as a teaching tool:

First, reconciliation, especially racial, is a *revelation*. Reconciliation is spiritually revealed. Like faith, it comes by hearing the Word of God repeatedly until we get it. Peter had to receive a supernatural revelation to be convinced that God was not a respecter of persons and that it was okay to mix the races. Cornelius's house was saved as a result.

The story of the prodigal son in Luke 15:11–32 is a perfect model of reconciliation. It is a complete record of how to be reconciled, and it begins with the revelation of four spiritual principles.

The first spiritual principle of the revelation of reconciliation is *repentance*: The prodigal son said, "I will arise and go to my father and say unto him, Father, I have sinned against *heaven,* and before *thee*" (v. 18 KJV, emphasis added). The son initiated the repentance that set up the forgiveness.

The second principle of the revelation of reconciliation is *forgiveness*: "But when he was yet a great way off, his father saw and had compassion, and ran, and fell on his neck, and kissed him" (v. 20 KJV). It seems to me that the father barely heard the son's repentance before overwhelming him with compassion and acts of forgiveness. The word *forgive* means "to cancel an obligation, such as a debt; the act of pardon." The operative word is *act;* forgiveness is most effective when it is included in an act.

The third principle of the revelation of reconciliation is *restoration*: "But the father said to his servants, Bring forth the best robe, and put it on him; and put a ring on his hand, and shoes on his feet" (v. 22 KJV). Restoration of what has been lost, whether relationally or materially, is a vital component of the act of forgiveness.

The fourth and final principle of the revelation of reconciliation is *celebration*: "And bring hither the fatted calf, and kill it; and let us eat and be merry" (v. 23 KJV). The celebration was the public announcement to all who witnessed the breakup that there had been a true reconciliation. It allowed the neighbors to see that the wayward son had returned, been forgiven, and restored and was evidenced by the father's giving him back his family status through the symbols of the ring and the robe.

It was revealed to the prodigal that he needed to go home to his father and repent. The Bible says, "He came to himself and said, 'I will arise.' " It was revealed to Simon Peter that it was all right to eat what had up to that time been forbidden by Jewish law. After his supernatural experience, Peter understood that the revelation concerned the error of considering as unclean a race different from his own. Racial reconciliation is a divine revelation that begins with one's reconciliation to God.

Second, racial reconciliation is *relational.* It is the restoration of a broken relationship between two or more people. The fractured relationship we have with God affects all other relationships. But 2 Corinthians 5:19 says, "God was reconciling the world to himself in Christ, not counting men's sins against them." Our relationship with the Father directly affects and extends to our relationships with others. God deputizes all believers and gives them the assignment of extending His peacemaking offer to nonbelievers: "And he has committed to us the message of reconciliation. We are therefore ambassadors, as though God were making his appeal through us. We implore you on Christ's behalf: Be reconciled to God" (2 Cor. 19–20).

The process takes place one-on-one. It is an individual revelation and experience that begins with a divine encounter and ends with a human encounter, and it leads to a contagious chain-reaction revival of relationships. The unexpected marvel of it all is that the relationships resulting from the acceptance of God's offer to be reconciled are live, real, and life changing. When I say yes to the deal, I am immediately affected, and the metamorphosis suggested in verse 17 is ignited: "Therefore, if anyone is in Christ he is a new creation; the old has gone, the new has come!" (2 Cor. 5:17).

That brings us to the third characteristic of racial reconciliation: it is *experiential*. Racial reconciliation is experiential, not experimental; therefore, we must not approach it as if we were experimenting with what is biblically mandated. It is experienced as a result of obedience to the Word of God. It is the work of faith as it relates to the healing and restoration of broken relationships. Since faith comes by hearing, and "hearing by the Word of God" (Rom. 10:17 KJV), reconciliation must be taught. Since faith without works is dead, it must be worked.

The ministry of reconciliation is experienced as we teach it and practice it, as it is walked out daily by the members of the body of Christ who accepted the offer of reconciliation with God through Christ. Reconciliation between God and humanity is a kingdom way of life. I am thoroughly convinced that the world will change only through the revelation imparted by the Word and the Holy Spirit to everyday relationships and the genuine experience that comes from obeying the Word of God.

Discussion Guide

1. Describe the three characteristics of biblical reconciliation discussed in this chapter. What would you add?

2. Describe how the reconciliation model of the prodigal son can be applied to racial reconciliation.

3. What roles do repentance and forgiveness play in the ministry of reconciliation?

4. In the twenty-first-century church, how necessary is the Acts 2 experience of the baptism in the Holy Spirit? What role might it play in racial reconciliation?

God of our Weary Years • *Dr. M. Tyrone Cushman*

Chapter 21

THIS TIME,
LET'S GET IT RIGHT

Let's get right down to the point. I suggest that we never again *intentionally* plan or plant a monocultural church, particularly in a multicultural community. Our seminaries should collaborate on promoting multiculturalism in the hearts and minds of every seminarian. Courses must be developed that teach us to minister to everybody, not just our own kind. Our churches should include a "claimer" in our bulletins that reads, "This church welcomes and desires to be home to the members of all races, nationalities, and colors, without exception or condition."

If the church of this generation wants to continue to preach unity as its cornerstone doctrine, it must put up or shut up. It must put its money and its best men and women in those places and projects that reflect that belief. We must absolutely stop trying to be politically correct and socially acceptable by the standards of a secular majority culture that is not moved by what moves the church—the Holy Spirit of God. Let the world see the church in all its beauty. Let us break free of our own fear and prejudice and release the power of God to change entire communities.

If I want to see the all-white suburban community evangelized, I should probably move into that suburb and work in a church there or plant one—not to integrate the community, but to evangelize it. Likewise, if you want to see the east side of Detroit won for the kingdom of God, you should probably move there and plant a church. If you are driven to use race as an excuse as to why God cannot use you, you are still in need of deliverance from the toxic conditioning of your past. By the way, that's okay. We've all been there and done that, one way or another. In a word, get over it! The bottom line is, you should never be allowed to govern where you do not dwell, and you will never be accepted as whole until you are a part.

Let us dwell together in accordance with Scripture. Let's stop playing games with words and study groups. Today's generation is neither ready nor willing to limit unity to fifth-Sunday Kodak moments held in candlelit atmospheres full of the sound of tear-jerking songs. Our young won't come, and even if they do come, they won't stay.

The generation that is content with token appointments and meaningless meetings is dead or dying. The next generation, black and white, is ready for change—now! The new millennium is demanding the demonstration of the Spirit and of power, even if it means starting new reformations.

Fresh Start

If we are serious about finding remedies for racism in the secular world and in the church, we must be serious about learning its origins and its causes, and we must be even more serious about discovering and applying solutions. Even so, the reality is that the solution is not going to be found in our beginnings and in our histories that blame a race or point a condemning finger at a particular generation.

As much as we might desire it, the solution will not come from a comprehensive intellectual understanding of God. The solution to racism in America and the world will come from embracing the gift of a fresh start that causes us to evaluate one another from an entirely new perspective and "not from a worldly point of view" (2 Cor. 5:16).

Here is the good news: we can indeed be reconciled to each other across racial, generational, gender, and economic lines if we will access the power of the resurrection of Jesus Christ. Anyone united with the Messiah gets a fresh start and is a new creation. "The old life is gone; the new life burgeons" (2 Cor. 5:17 MSG).

The church's *only* job is to be the ambassador of the message of reconciliation, which, according to 2 Corinthians 5:19, is "Come on home; God is not holding your sins against you." That's it! We must extend to one another what has been extended to us — an unconditional offer of a fresh start.

This is not a new revelation. Reconciliation is as old as the written Word itself. But the church has been infiltrated by secular spirits and corrupted by an age of reason where men value their secular intelligence above the holy Word of God. Sadly, instead of the church being the solution, it stepped outside of its kingdom purpose and became the problem.

Racism finds its power and origin in the spirit of division, a demonic spirit that manifests itself as racism, sexism, classism, denominationalism, and the like. There must, therefore, be an antidote that is far reaching, completely inclusive, and everlasting. Only one comes to mind — His name is Jesus.

The New Race

A new power minority must rise up in the name of Jesus and claim territory (people's hearts and minds) for God. God's kingdom must come, if civility is to reign. The kingdom of God is established on earth as believers multiply and become militant for kingdom rule and kingdom rules that will dispossess the kingdom of darkness. The church must engage in the battle for the establishment of God's kingdom principles and not merely focus on its own survival, its doctrinal debates, or the divisiveness of its right-left politics that contradicts our stated purpose and further encourages the world to ignore us.

Here is a scary thought for some: we must separate ourselves from the notion that the church will triumph through democracies where majorities rule and where we Christians exercise the political power that forces non-Christians to act and look like us. We must not forget that we are Christians because we are redeemed by the blood sacrifice of Jesus Christ—not because we are Republicans or Democrats. We are Christians because we have taken the deal and freely chosen to believe. We are Christians in spite of our politics—not because of our politics.

We take dominion over the earth through the power of the Spirit of God, which is the power of love, unity, and reconciliation—not the power of a vote. Ours is a theocracy; that is, rule by God, not by a majority. We do not win because we have the numbers; we win in spite of the numbers, because we are on the winning side.

Listen to what the apostle Paul wrote to the Corinthian church:

> The world is unprincipled. It's dog-eat-dog out there! The world doesn't fight fair. But we don't live or fight our battles that way—never have and never will. The tools of our trade aren't for marketing or manipulation, but they are for demolishing that entire massively corrupt culture. We use our powerful God-tools for smashing warped philosophies, tearing down barriers erected against the truth of God, fitting every loose thought and emotion and impulse into the

structure of life shaped by Christ. Our tools are ready at hand for clearing the ground of every obstruction and building lives of obedience into maturity.

—2 Corinthians 10:2-6 MSG

We cannot stake claim to spiritual territory by intellectual means. In the kingdom of God, we are neither beholden to nor dependent upon majorities for victory. The kingdom of God rules as it renews minds through transformation, not political or even religious reformations. Otherwise, the church is reduced to a mere religious institution serving its own end and gaining political advantage by lobbying Congress and bribing politicians. Competing with other secular institutions for numerical control, it is thus rendered powerless and offers a morality that must always win a popularity contest.

Let's keep it real. Let's not allow the world to squeeze us into its mold and cause us to look like cold, mean, cranky, judgmental, war-mongering freaks. I choose to be as gentle as Jesus and to offer covering to those caught in the act of sin. I choose to be as salty as the Savior when I find religious people conning the poor and unsuspecting right inside the church. Somebody hand me a stick!

I have decided I can win more people through a demonstration of God's love than through demonizing their bad choices. Jesus is the prime example of patience, forbearance, tolerance, and understanding. As I grow spiritually, I want to be like Him.

Discussion Guide

1. How intentional must the church be in reflecting the Bible's teachings regarding race and gender issues? How can it demonstrate what it believes?

2. Who is the new power minority?

3. When, if ever, is militancy appropriate as a method in the church?

4. Is there a right way and is there a wrong way to win?

God of our Weary Years • Dr. M. Tyrone Cushman

Chapter 22

THE DEMONSTRATION OF SPIRIT AND POWER

Show and Tell

When John the Baptist sent word to Jesus, asking, "Are you the one who was to come, or should we expect someone else?" Jesus answered, "Go back and report to John what you hear and see: The blind receive sight, the lame walk, those who have leprosy are cured, the deaf hear, the dead are raised and the good news is preached to the poor" (Matt. 11:3, 4–5). The following is my personal show-and-tell experience. It is my report of what I have seen and heard.

Place for Life

Recently Jackie and I decided to visit a church we had heard about. We had visited a couple of churches in search of the one that would be a perfect fit. Since I had been a veteran senior pastor for almost forty years and the former general overseer of my denomination, we had a good idea of what we needed and an even better idea of what we did not need — ever again — in life.

We were sure we did not want to be where Roberts Rules of Order governed anything. Though we do not believe in abortion, we discovered we did not want to be around people who cared more about overturning *Roe v. Wade* than helping young women to be reconciled to God and discover their purpose in spite of their mess. We knew we did not want to be caught up in church fights, fusses, traditionalism, or extremism — ever again.

We knew we wanted to be where the whole Bible was preached and practiced; where worship was fresh, real, and dynamic; and where we could be relatively sure that every Sunday we would be fed with a relevant word. We did not care about size. We just wanted to be in His presence.

Jackie had become weary of going to church but coming home spiritually hungry and was still recovering from past bruises that turn weaker pilgrims away from God and church forever. In an effort to perk up her spirits, I agreed to go with her to a nine o'clock service on the west side recommended by my niece Theresa. In turn, Jackie agreed to attend an eleven o'clock service across town at a lovely little church pastored by one of my spiritual sons. We were not prepared to find the perfect fit, but it happened.

At the nine o'clock service, we were greeted at the door by several people of different races who hugged and welcomed us so warmly that Jackie asked me if I knew them. As we entered the sanctuary, we received a second wave of handshakes and hugs. We took seats center front and waited for the service to begin.

We immediately noticed the contemporary stage set, the lights, and the state-of-the-art sound system. I'm a high-tech freak, so I had one foot in heaven already. Worship began, and without anyone giving instruction, everyone immediately stood to their feet. It was instant, unanimous, and powerful. The choir was racially mixed, and they looked like they were having a great time. The minister of music exhorted the audience with passion and excitement. The thumping rhythm made me want to dance.

As I looked around, I noticed the racial makeup. It was a rather even spread of approximately fifteen hundred black, white, and Hispanic people, many leaping, dancing, singing, and shouting. For a Church of God boy, accustomed to either all-black or all white congregations, this was fascinating.

The music was powerful, and the Spirit and presence of God were heavy. At prayer time there was an invitation to come forward for prayer. Hundreds came — all colors. The deacons and elders were male and female and, again, all races. They met the people, laid their hands on them, prayed for them, and sent them back to their seats. It seemed unrushed and very efficient. Jackie, who is legally blind, leaned over and asked me if the pastor was black or white. I told her I didn't know.

When it was time for the preaching, a white man in his late forties or early fifties came out in bibbed overalls. He later explained that the overalls would help him demonstrate the word God had given him. He was very confident and spoke with a strong Cajun accent, causing my wife to think he was black. "No, honey," I whispered, "he's very white."

His subject dealt with the principles of plowing. Forty-five minutes later, we found ourselves weeping at the altar. We returned to our seats. The pastor gave what we now know is his signature benediction: "Success to you — success to the kingdom of God." We sat down, looking at each other. Stunned, I said, "Jackie . . .," and as people married for forty years often do, she finished my sentence, ". . . I think this is what we were looking for."

As the weeks went by, each Wednesday-night Bible study and Sunday-morning worship service left us literally in tears and with our mouths hanging open in exclamation. For sure, much of our reaction was a result of what we had come through and where we had come from. We were like two thirsty pilgrims crawling out of a dry, hot desert into an oasis with a cool, satisfying stream. We had found the proverbial stream in the desert.

Past experience notwithstanding, I believe we have experienced what the New Testament church of God looks and feels like. It is loving, warm, worship oriented, Christ centered, Word focused, kingdom based, multicultural, Spirit filled, evangelistic, happy, inclusive, and very, very encouraging.

And this wonderful place that we found is Place for Life in San Antonio, Texas, led by Bishop Rick Hawkins.

Abundant Life Christian Fellowship

Abundant Life Christian Fellowship, led by Pastor Paul E. Sheppard of Palo Alto, California, is phenomenal in its growth (over four thousand and still growing) and its multicultural membership. I think every race and nationality under the sun attends Abundant Life. Pastor Paul also sponsors *Enduring Truth,* perhaps the fastest-growing radio program in America.

It has been my honor to speak to this awesome fellowship. The fact that I have known Pastor Paul and his family from his childhood has made his success no less amazing to me. We came from the same roots, and those roots were nothing like what I have experienced at Abundant Life.

Covenant Church of Pittsburgh

Covenant Church of Pittsburgh is led by Bishop Joseph Garlington, who is by far the most gifted man of God that I have ever met. His church is a multicultural congregation of several thousand and sponsors a reconciliation network that impacts hundreds of thousands around the world. The presence and power of God in Covenant Church of Pittsburgh is beyond description. I have highlighted Covenant Church, as well as the two previously mentioned churches, as modern marvels and models of God's kingdom on earth. There are many more, and there is a growing number of men and women of God who have determined to have nothing less than the authentic New Testament expression of God's kingdom.

As I have mentioned earlier, many churches are monocultural because their communities tend to be monocultural. In and of itself, that is not wrong; it is simply an expression of geographical realities. For example, Bishop Timothy J. Clarke in Columbus, Ohio, pastors an exciting but predominantly black church with more than six thousand members. However, he remains dedicated to racial reconciliation and multiculturalism.

This unique phenomenon is especially true in the inner city. Some of the most effective churches in the inner cities are predominantly white, others are predominantly black, and still others are predominantly Hispanic; but in each case, the church is totally dedicated to the issues that support other races and even other denominations. They all are New Testament representatives of the kingdom of God, and they indeed represent it very well.

That the World May Believe

Twenty-first-century credibility among religious institutions will be determined by a demonstration of Spirit and of power. Technology has given the world instant global access to truth and deception alike. In this age, both fraudulent claims and true power can be quickly revealed.

As Elijah said to the prophets of Baal, "Let the god who answers by fire be God." I say to each of you that the true New Testament church of God is the church where the blind receive sight, the lame walk, those who have leprosy are cured, the deaf hear, the dead are raised, and the good news is preached to the poor. I don't know about you, but I want to be part of a congregation that reflects those attributes.

Our diversity notwithstanding, Christian denominations are all parts of the whole. None of us is the whole, and even if denominational or reformational subgroups combine their parts, they still do not constitute the whole. We must endeavor to keep the unity of the body, the kingdom of God, by coordinating, cooperating, and sharing what we have in common even as we work within our separate traditions and unique emphases.

I repeat, our greater challenge is to be reconciled with all Christians, not merely all Christians in the same denomination. Are we as ready to mix with other Christians as we are with other races? It's a question worth asking. Most of us are convinced that racial segregation is not of God. But what about denominationalism, where theology segregates blood-bought brothers and sisters? Do we find ourselves saying to the sheep of other folds what Peter said when he was ordered by a heavenly vision to rise and eat: "Surely not, Lord! I have never eaten anything impure or unclean"?

The same voice that spoke to Peter speaks to you and me: "Do not call anything impure that God has made clean." Peter's revelation was life changing for him and is no less so for us. He confessed in Acts 10:34–35: "I now realize how true it is that God does not show favoritism but accepts men from every nation who fear him and do what is right." That too should be our confession.

An Abiding Commitment

I am confident that God is moving on the hearts of many of us who are part of reformation movements and religious revolutions of one kind or another. There is a growing conviction that racial unity is not merely the politically correct and fashionable thing to do, but the right thing to do, and it brings liberation to us all. God's people are ready to make an abiding commitment that will position the church to experience new and wonderful gifts and graces that allow them to live and operate as God's ambassadors.

I am in constant dialogue with the men and women in the trenches. I believe my fellow reconcilers will concur with me that we have an ever-decreasing window of opportunity to counteract the elements that threaten to destroy our witness and influence as we know it. Someone has said, "The opportunity of a lifetime must be seized in the lifetime of the opportunity." Because it is time to advance the kingdom of God, I am compelled to do whatever it takes to seize the opportunity to build bridges that link our parts.

As leaders of any group, we must seek to build bridges over the ever-increasing generational divide and bridges that link and liberate race, culture, nationality, and gender. Let us all pledge to let nothing separate us from the love of God.

Linking Generations

I have dear friends who are pastoring churches with budgets larger than the denominational organizations of which they are members. Many of them are frustrated from fighting the wars of their fathers: political battles over titles, traditions, and doctrine. They have outgrown their denomination's usefulness and have received scorn and endured great criticism for singing new songs and preaching a more relevant gospel.

Persuading this new breed of men and women to remain in organizations that they perceive do not want them is much like trying to convince a battered wife to stay in a marriage in the hope that her husband will someday stop beating her. These cutting-edge leaders do not want to wrestle or fight their fathers for a place at the table. Yet I believe they were born for this hour and have been brought forth in the kingdom at this precise time to lead the next generation with a fresh apostolic anointing.

My dearest friend, Bishop Gideon Thompson, is one of the most outstanding teachers and preachers in this country and pastors one of the largest and most effective churches in New England. Despite his obvious anointing and success, he was deleted from the approved-ministers list of our denomination because he did not consistently attend the regional ministers' meetings. As a result, his church of several thousand was penalized, left out of the yearbook, and his credentials threatened by a small fellowship of churches whose combined congregations numbered less than two hundred members.

These young warriors, male and female, are leading thousands and impacting tens of thousands around the world. Should they be brought before tribunals and credentialing committees to be judged by men who do not know them and have never experienced their level of effectiveness? Or should we make room for them, learn from them, and celebrate with them? The answer is obvious. Let's get on with it!

From the Mouths of Babes

I believe the church has veered off course by emphasizing a parochial unity, one that emphasizes intradenominational agreement while ignoring the broader interdenominational fellowship with sheep of other folds. Our organizational or denominational witness, however, is not nearly as important as our overall Christian witness. Preaching the kingdom of God and walking in a real-time and real-life demonstration of Spirit and power will grow the church at both ends: the grassroots level and the organizational level.

Demonstration trumps denomination every time! Recently I received an e-mail from a young minister that said: "Church was powerful on Sunday. The anointing was so strong that Pastor Kidd didn't even get a chance to preach. He began to prophesy to people in the congregation and pray for them. It was one of the most powerful services I have ever been a part of."

There it was again: that pattern that intrudes and imposes on open hearts and church bulletins. Where the Word and the Spirit operate together, God is present in power, and as a result, the blind see, the lame walk, the deaf hear, the dead are raised, and the gospel is preached to the poor. This young minister had touched the hem of His garment and was healed of the disease of religion. I prayed, "Oh God, may he and Pastor Kidd never turn back."

Discussion Guide

1. What is your show-and-tell experience regarding the move of God in the church world today?

2. What would be a balanced, winning, and godly approach to bridge building?

3. Demonstration trumps _____. Which is most attractive to you, and why?

4. Which is the more effective method for achieving interdenominational unity: from the top down (organizational) or from the bottom up (local church to local church)? What makes this method superior to the other?

Chapter 23

BACK TO THE FUTURE

In concluding this book, I wish to offer four practical suggestions that, if applied, will help restore the church's legitimacy, purpose, and perhaps even its spiritual integrity. With these four suggestions, we can harness new paradigms that reflect the shift that has already occurred in the heavens.

God is indeed doing a new thing, and tremendous change is already underway. But I believe we are being called to embrace the principles that will take us forward. We are being called to adapt and shift with God if we want to make a difference in the new millennium.

Getting Over Ourselves

First, I believe as church people, we must get over ourselves. We must resist the temptation to worship heritage, and we must remember that our denominations and movements were a means to an end—not the end itself. We must honor the past and glean from it the foundational truths that matter without getting stuck there.

In the apostle Paul's second letter to the Corinthians, he declared, "So from now on we will regard no one from a worldly point of view. Though we once regarded Christ in this way, we do so no longer" (2 Cor. 5:16). We must ask God for a fresh humility that includes and accepts the "least of these." Too often the way we have regarded ourselves, others, and Jesus has often turned the good news to bad and twisted a wonderful organization with a message of life into a deaf and dumb monolithic monument.

Together we must declare the spirit of division broken! Together we must declare that our best days are in front of us and not behind. Together we must declare our future will be greater than our past. Together we must restore the grace-based message of the New Testament: "whosoever will, let him come."

God is still moving, forming, and reforming us into His likeness. He is working through men and women of diverse origins and understandings; and through the miracle work of His Holy Spirit, we are encouraged to be "completely humble and gentle; be patient, bearing with one another in love. Make every effort to keep the unity of the Spirit through the bond of peace" (Eph. 4:2–3).

Contrary to popular and self-serving religious opinions, God is not funneling Himself or all the world's cultures, races, or nationalities through one narrow denomination, movement, or religion. If we are to have any credibility at all, we *must* acknowledge that God is moving in the world through many different movements. When we acknowledge that fact, we will be free to accept diversity—culturally, theologically, doctrinally, and organizationally. But first, we must get over ourselves.

Restoring the Power of Pentecost

Second, we must restore the power of Pentecost and reestablish the preeminence of the Holy Spirit. Worship and prayer are the ushers to Pentecost or supernatural visitation. If we are to experience the power of the early church, we must recapture the Spirit of Acts 2:1–4. We must encourage renewals and revivals that promote prayer and worship all over the world at levels unseen in this generation. It is time to turn loose the prayer warriors and the intercessors! It's time to issue a call for the weeping women to travail that Zion might bring forth again! It is time to free the gifts and the gifted!

Let us pray for a fresh outpouring of the Holy Spirit. Let us declare a solemn assembly that we might be freshly anointed to preach the Word in power and demonstration and that we might be empowered by His Spirit to exercise dominion. This is the way God rules His kingdom through us.

We must lose our fear of the Holy Spirit and release Him to be active in our worship experience. We absolutely must free the gifts of the Spirit. They are the weaponry and tools that enable the body of Christ—despite its complexities and diversity in members, polity, history, and heritage—to live united, wage war, occupy enemy territory, and facilitate the dominion of the kingdom of God on earth.

The Holy Spirit is the missing link in the power chain that connects us as individuals and bonds us to our purpose as the collective body of Christ. The power of resurrection that raised Jesus from the dead is the same power that takes men and women from death unto life and breaks the yoke of sin and all its manifestations—including the sin of racism. It is the power spoken of by the apostle Paul in Philippians 3:10: "I want to know Christ and the power of his resurrection and the fellowship of sharing in his suffering, becoming like him in his death, and so, somehow to attain to the resurrection from the dead."

It is the job of the Holy Spirit to empower the believer to become what God says he can be and to do what God has called him to do. This is precisely why the disciples were told, "Do not leave Jerusalem, but wait for the gift my Father promised, which you have heard me speak about. For John baptized with water, but in a few days you will be baptized with the Holy Spirit" (Acts 1:4–5). The Holy Spirit is indispensable to the life and work of the church. Absolutely nothing lives, lasts, or changes without His enabling power.

The Holy Spirit and the Word create the primary difference between cold, dead religion ruled by men and the kingdom of God ruled by God through men. The

Spirit and the Word are God's witnesses on the earth, indwelling believers who then embody the purpose and power of the kingdom of God. We receive this power only when the Holy Spirit indwells or "comes on" us: "But you will receive power when the Holy Spirit comes on you; and you will be my witnesses in Jerusalem, and in all Judea and Samaria, and to the ends of the earth" (Acts 1:8).

One of the most virulent poisons to the body of Christ is the diabolic divisiveness of racism. The only antidote for it is the enabling power promised and received on the day of Pentecost, which is the baptism of the Holy Spirit. The unity that results from the bonding power of the Holy Spirit enables the church to be God's witness on the earth, while the disunity that results in spiritual impotence is the church's Achilles heel. It's worth mentioning again the words of the psalmist: "How good and pleasant it is when brothers live together in unity! . . . For there the Lord bestows his blessing, even life forevermore" (Ps. 133:1, 3).

Knowing how critical the unity of believers would be for the kingdom, Jesus, God in the flesh, prayed:

My prayer is not for them alone. I pray also for those who will believe in me through their message, that all of them may be one, Father, just as you are in me and I am in you. May they also be in us so that the world may believe that you have sent me. I have given them the glory that you gave me, that they may be one as we are one:

I in them and you in me. May they be brought
to complete unity to let the world know that you
sent me and have loved them even as you have
loved me.

—John 17:20–23

Without the Holy Spirit, the church will lose
its relevancy, grovel for secular favor, and settle for
mere religious coexistence. In the name of God, it
will compromise its purpose as it makes self-serving
political deals diluting its purpose, destroying its unity,
and neutralizing its witness. It is not an option; we must
return to our life source, the Holy Spirit.

Be Joined

Third, we must be joined to one another in every
way possible. Our orders are clear: "Be completely
humble and gentle; be patient, bearing with one another
in love. Make every effort to keep the unity of the Spirit
through the bond of peace. There is one body and one
Spirit—just as you were called to one hope when you
were called—one Lord, one faith, one baptism; one God
and Father of all, who is over all and through all and in
all" (Eph. 4:2–6).

A dear friend of mine, Dr. Curtiss Paul DeYoung,
is the lead author of a powerful collaborative work with
Michael O. Emerson, George Yancey, and Karen Chai
Kim entitled *United by Faith — The Multiracial Congregation
as an Answer to the Problem of Race*. In the section called

"Arguing the Case for Multiracial Congregations," they write:

> While racial separation may be sociologically comfortable, we do not accept it as ordained by God. According to the Bible, in the beginning God created one race, the human race (Genesis 1:26–27). Jesus and the first-century church believed they were commissioned to create congregations that more accurately reflected God's original intention for the human family. The day of Pentecost birthed a multicultural church that served as a re-creation of God's original intention. Racial separation in the United States is socially constructed. The church in the United States reflects a social reality rather than promoting a theological vision. . . . We believe that churches should be committed to dealing with one of the most important moral issues of this day — racism — and must work toward producing racial reconciliation. To this end, even if it seems that multiracial churches are not pragmatic, churches should have important transcendent concerns that make the work toward racially integrated congregations valuable. (p. 131)

Not only do I concur with Dr. DeYoung and his team, but I prophetically assert that multiracial church planting is twenty-first-century evangelism. We must go out of our way to make other cultures feel welcomed and included. It is our call. We must learn one another's ways and endure one another's excesses as we enjoy, or at least endure, one another's gifts, talents, and service. We must declare a new openness and inclusiveness. We must back away from our growing tendency to exclude those whose doctrinal and theological emphases are different from our own.

I invite each of you to become a covenant member of other groups that are open to receive you. Extend yourself. Step beyond mono- and become bi-, tri-, and even quad-cultural. Try not to get all your cultural education from the news media. (The mainstream media is all about marketing, not truth.) Let us all—black, brown, yellow, white, and all shades in between—resist thinking in the vacuum of monocultural proclivities and racially biased predispositions.

One Church, Many Ministries

Fourth, let us embrace the notion of one church with many ministries and remove the threat that one of us has to lose his or her heritage for unity to exist. It is silly to ask me to give up my land, my history, my heritage, and my inheritance while you keep yours. That is not going to happen. I should not have to die for you to live. God sent Jesus, not me, to die for our sins. We must not continue to victimize the victim in order to fix the problem.

In all my research, the most positive and replicable example of the churches potential to heal itself and the world it is sent to was found in what Dr. Vinson Synan calls The Memphis Miracle. It is a 21st century model of racial and denominational reconciliation:

> When the delegates arrived in Memphis on October 17, 1994, there was an electric air of expectation that something wonderful was about to happen. The conference theme was Pentecostal Partners: A Reconciliation Strategy for 21st Century Ministry. Over 3,000 persons attended the evening sessions in the Dixon-Meyers Hall of the Cook Convention Center in downtown Memphis. Everyone was aware of the racial strife in Memphis where Martin Luther King, Jr. was assassinated in 1968. Here, it was hoped, a great racial healing would take place. The night services reflected the tremendous work done by the local committee in the months before the gathering. Bishop Gilbert Patterson of the Temple of Deliverance Church of God in Christ, and Samuel Middlebrook, Pastor of the Raleigh Assembly of God in Memphis, co-chaired the committee. Although both men had pastored in the same city for 29 years, they had never met. The Memphis project brought them together.
>
> The morning sessions were remarkable for the honesty and candor of the papers that were presented by a team of leading Pentecostal scholars. These included Dr. Cecil M. Robeck, Jr. of Fuller Theological Seminary and the Assemblies of God, Dr. Leonard Lovett of the Church of God in Christ, Dr. William Turner of Duke University and the United Holy Church, and Dr. Vinson Synan of Regent University

and the Pentecostal Holiness Church. In these sessions, the sad history of separation, racism and neglect was laid bare before the 1,000 or more leaders assembled. These sometimes chilling confessions brought a stark sense of past injustice and the absolute need of repentance and reconciliation. The evening worship sessions were full of Pentecostal fire and fervor as Bishop Patterson, Billy Joe Daugherty and Jack Hayford preached rousing sermons to the receptive crowds.

The climactic moment, however, came in the scholars session on the afternoon of October 18, after Bishop Blake tearfully told the delegates, Brothers and Sisters, I commit my love to you. There are problems down the road, but a strong commitment to love will overcome them all. Suddenly there was a sweeping move of the Holy Spirit over the entire assembly. A young black brother uttered a spirited message in tongues after which Jack Hayford hurried to the microphone to give the interpretation. He began by saying, For the Lord would speak to you this day, by the tongue, by the quickening of the Spirit, and he would say:

My sons and my daughters, look if you will from the heavenward side of things, and see where you have been , two, separate streams, that is, streams as at flood tide. For I have poured out of my Spirit upon you and flooded you with grace in both your circles of gathering and fellowship. But as streams at flood tide, nonetheless, the waters have been muddied to some degree. Those of desperate thirst have come, nonetheless, for muddy water is better than none at all.

My sons and my daughters, if you will look and see that there are some not come to drink because of what they have seen. You have not been aware of it, for only heaven has seen those who would doubt what flowed in your midst, because of the waters muddied having been soiled by the clay of your humanness, not by your crudity, lucidity, or intentionality, but by the clay of your humanness the river has been made impure.

But look. Look, for I, by my Spirit, am flowing the two streams into one. And the two becoming one, if you can see from the heaven side of things, are being purified and not only is there a new purity coming in your midst, but there will be multitudes more who will gather at this one mighty river because they will see the purity of the reality of my love manifest in you. And so, know that as heaven observes and tells us what is taking place, there is reason for you to rejoice and prepare yourself for here shall be multitudes more than ever before come to this joint surging of my grace among you, says the Lord.

Immediately, a white pastor appeared in the wings of the backstage with a towel and basin of water. His name was Donald Evans, an Assemblies of God pastor from Tampa, Florida. When he explained that the Lord had called him to wash the feet of a black leader as a sign of repentance, he was given access to the platform. In a moment of tearful contrition, he washed the feet of Bishop Clemmons while begging forgiveness for the sins of the whites against their black brothers and sisters. A wave of weeping swept over the auditorium. Then, Bishop Blake approached Thomas Trask, General Superintendent of the Assemblies of God, and tearfully washed his feet as a sign of repentance for any animosity blacks had harbored against their white brothers and sisters. This was the climatic moment of the conference. Everyone sensed that this was the final seal of Holy Spirit approval from the heart of God over the proceedings. In an emotional speech the next day, Dr. Paul Walker of the Church of God (Cleveland, TN) called this event, the Miracle in Memphis, a name that stuck and made headlines around the world.

That afternoon, the members of the old PFNA gathered for the final session of its history. In a very short session, a motion was carried to dissolve the old, all-white organization in favor of a new entity that would be birthed the next day. But more reconciliation was yet to come!

When the new constitution was read to the delegates on October 19, a new name was proposed for he group-Pentecostal Churches of North America (PCNA). It was suggested that the governing board of the new group have equal numbers of blacks and whites and that denominational charter memberships would be welcomed that very day. But before the constitution came before the assembly for a vote, Pastor Billy Joe Daugherty of Tulsa's Victory Christian Center asked the delegates to include the word Charismatic in the new name. Over a hastily-called luncheon meeting of the Restructuring Committee, it was agreed that those Christians who thought of themselves as Charismatics would also be invited to join. When the vote was taken, the body unanimously voted to call the new organization the Pentecostal and Charismatic Churches of North America (PCCNA). Thus the Memphis Miracle included the beginning of healing between Pentecostals and Charismatics as well as between blacks and whites.

Another milestone of the day was the unanimous adoption of a Racial Reconciliation Manifesto that was drafted by Bishop Ithiel Clemmons, Dr. Cecil M. Robeck, Jr., Dr. Leonard Lovett, and Dr. Harold D. Hunter. In this historic document, the new PCCNA pledged to oppose racism prophetically in all its various manifestations and to be vigilant in the struggle. They further agreed to confess that racism is a sin and as a blight must be condemned while promising to seek partnerships and exchange pulpits with persons of a different hue in the spirit of our Blessed Lord who prayed that we might be one.

After this, the election of officers took place with Bishop Clemmons chosen as Chairman and Bishop Underwood as Vice-Chairman. Also elected to the Board was Bishop Barbara Amos, whose election demonstrated the resolve of the new organization to bridge the gender gap as well. The other officers represented a balance of blacks and whites from the constituent membership. [Miracle and Mandate; By Dr. Vinson Synan; IPHC Archives and Research Center (digital library:arc.iphc.org) The Online Journal: PCCNA NEWS; Memphis, TN.; October, 1994]

If fostering true unity requires dissolution and starting anew from scratch (my personal preference), then *everybody* should dissolve and *everybody* should sell everything. If blending memberships is the answer, then let *everybody* be joined, and let the celebration of the beauty of holiness, diversity, and true unity begin. Using the New Testament church as the model, let us sell or share all that we have and create a new dwelling place where we will share all things in common and where there is a live demonstration of the Spirit and power.

I believe that the kingdom of God is poised to empower the church toward genuine spiritual and ecclesiastical breakthrough. As dialogue is supported by an expanding sphere of leaders in apostolic (New Testament) alignment exercising apostolic authority, we will see a fresh move of the Spirit of God and a unity that, in the words of the psalmist, will be "good and pleasant." I pray that as we speak, our words will provoke hope and ignite discussion and rediscovery of the kingdom purpose for which we were called and created.

The Ultimate Strategy: Covenants of Unconditional Love

We are well able to overcome the scourge of racism and its mother, the spirit of division. However, we must be willing to look at ourselves and understand how we have been shaped by events that preceded us. As uncomfortable as it may be, we must acknowledge that the perpetuation of privilege is instinctive but leads only to the generational transmission of a dark DNA based on majority-race membership that devalues others.

In the midst of all this, we must look unflinchingly at one another without turning away from the raw, unsightly realities, and we must allow ourselves to be reconciled by that unconditional love that comes only from God. We absolutely must have courageous conversations that conclude with unconditional, multiracial community covenants of caring and sharing.

As corny as it may sound, the application of unconditional love is now our most powerful weapon and only hope. The power of good is the power of God and when applied without respect to race religion, gender, or national origin, it always overcomes evil.

The power of good is not manifested in our politics or the polarizing labels of "liberal" and "conservative." The power of good over evil is manifested only in our love applied . . . in real time . . . on real people . . . one community at a time.

God of our weary years,
God of our silent tears,
Thou who has brought us thus far on the way;
Thou who has by Thy might
Led us into the light,
Keep us forever in the path, we pray.
Lest our feet stray from the places, our God, where we met Thee,
Lest our hearts, drunk with the wine of the world, we forget Thee;
Shadowed beneath Thy hand,
May we forever stand,
True to our God,
True to our native land.

Success to you, and success to the kingdom of God!

Discussion Guide

1. What do we mean when we say we must go back to the future?

2. What are the four principles that can revive, restore, and relaunch the church of the new millennium?

3. What is God's ultimate strategy for His victorious church?

4. What does an unconditional love covenant look like? If you were writing a covenant statement between yourself and a person of another race what would it be?

Contact the Author:

Dr. M. Tyrone Cushman
3307 Buckhaven Drive
San Antonio, TX 78230
(210) 602-3894
tyronecushman@mac.com